Revivalism, Social Conscience, and
Community in the Burned-Over District

Revivalism, Social Conscience, and Community in the Burned-Over District

THE TRIAL OF RHODA BEMENT

Glenn C. Altschuler

AND

Jan M. Saltzgaber

CORNELL UNIVERSITY PRESS

ITHACA AND LONDON

First published 1983 by Cornell University Press.
First printing, Cornell Paperbacks, 1983
Published in the United Kingdom by Cornell University Press Ltd.,
Ely House, 37 Dover Street, London W1X 4HQ.

International Standard Book Number (cloth) 0-8014-1541-1
International Standard Book Number (paper) 0-8014-9246-7
Library of Congress Catalog Card Number 82-14296
Printed in the United States of America
Librarians: Library of Congress cataloging information appears on the last page of the book.

The paper in this book is acid-free and meets the guidelines for permanence and durability of the Committee on Production Guidelines for Book Longevity of the Council on Library Resources.

Contents

Illustrations

Map

Preface

In this small book we attempt to build a world, the world of a rural village in antebellum New York State, around a single document. Our text is the trial of Rhoda Bement by the Session of the First Presbyterian Church of Seneca Falls, New York. Bement was accused of "unchristian and unladylike" conduct in challenging the authority of her minister for his refusal to announce abolitionist lectures from the pulpit. Her trial took place in 1843, a moment when both her church and her community were particularly vulnerable. While still buffeted by the economic uncertainty that followed the Panic of 1837, the people of Seneca Falls—indeed, of much of America—were caught up in a wave of religious enthusiasm and reform activity which posed new threats to an often fragile sense of community. The transcript of the Bement trial provides an extraordinary glimpse of the complex relationship between revivalism, which often pricked the social consciences of converts, and such antebellum reform movements as abolitionism, the temperance crusade, and the call for women's rights. It shows that those who embraced revivalism did not necessarily endorse social reforms and that those who sympathized with a particular reform often disagreed sharply over the means of introducing it. Throughout, the transcript demonstrates that the ideal of a stable community was a powerful counterweight to the mounting pressures for change.

The participants in the trial, although perhaps more prosperous than many of their neighbors, are ordinary men and women who reflect in considerable measure the stresses of the times. They are not posing before the eye of history, and their very lack of a sense of historical import gives their testimony a powerful immediacy. They were people accustomed to speaking their consciences in intimate units such as the family, the church congregation, and the community. Since the trial threatened the integrity of one of these units, its transcript is a record of the participants' most fundamental concerns, one that adds significantly to our understanding of that center of New York State revivalism known as the Burned-Over District.

The transcript of the trial, here annotated and presented in its entirety, is the dramatic centerpiece of this book. To provide a context in which to read and interpret the trial, we have written two essays. The first, by Jan Saltzgaber, sets the stage by examining the religious and social ramifications of the Second Great Awakening in the "burned-over" region of New York. He analyzes in detail the changing social and economic environment of Seneca Falls and clearly delineates connections between these changes and the currents of revival and reform in the 1830s and 1840s. In the second essay Glenn Altschuler uses the trial and evidence from other local churches to reassess the divisive tendencies of revivalism. Altschuler stresses local conditions and church practices that acted as centripetal forces, forces that impressed conservatives, moderates, and even "ultraists" with the importance of church unity. The threat of disintegration and schism, constantly exacerbated by the social, economic, and religious tensions of the period, deeply troubled Protestants who sought ways to satisfy their consciences without destroying the bulwark of social order and Christian piety. Indeed, all three parts of the book support our view that organized religion was central to the stability and cohesiveness of village life in antebellum America.

This book reflects the mandate of the National Endowment for the Humanities grant that led to our study of Seneca Falls.

Preface

We were charged with the task of locating, collecting, and making available the neglected and endangered records of religious congregations throughout western New York. We believe that the inaccessibility of local historical documents has led to some serious misunderstandings of antebellum America. This book makes a small contribution to righting this situation; we hope it will find a place not only on the bookshelves of readers but in the classroom as well.

Thanking friends and colleagues is a delightful duty. To the Session of the Presbyterian Church of Seneca Falls and the Reverend William Knox we owe our greatest debt, not only for permission to publish this document, but for making time, space, and their expertise available to us. The staff of the Seneca Falls Historical Society scoured the community for information, introduced us to countless people in the locality, and patiently responded to what must have seemed an endless series of requests. The Bement trial was located and microfilmed through a grant by the National Endowment for the Humanities, and we join the ranks of thousands of historians in expressing our gratitude to this indispensable agency and its staff. Thanks are due as well to the American Antiquarian Society, Worcester, Massachusetts; the Amistad Research Center, New Orleans, Louisiana; the Seneca Falls Historical Society, Seneca Falls, New York; and the Wayne County Historical Society, Lyons, New York—all of which gave us permission to quote from materials in their collections. Finally, we thank the Department of Manuscripts and University Archives, Cornell University Libraries, Cornell University, for permission to quote from the church records in their collection listed under accession numbers 3631, 6003, 6005, 6007, 6017, 6020, 6021, 6038, and 6118.

Colleagues, students, and friends remind us that the term "community of scholars" can be a pleasant and enlightening reality. Miriam Brody read the text of the trial, providing encouragement and enormously helpful suggestions as to how it might best be presented. Gary Bagley, Todd Bernstein, Eric

11

Kotcher, and Mark C. Lamphier began as research assistants and have become friends. A. S. Eisenstadt, Michael Kammen, R. Laurence Moore, Linda Nelson, Don Scott, and Joel Silbey read and criticized an earlier version of Glenn Altschuler's essay with their customary skill and sympathy. Bernhard Kendler, as always, is a discerning editor who is a pleasure to work with. John Ackerman, a superb copy editor, punched our prose without bruising our egos. Lana Morse served as typist, editor, and unflagging comrade.

Finally, we thank each other. Historians, we believe, tend all too often to work in an unsplendid isolation. We have satisfied ourselves that two heads are much better than one and that collaboration can make scholarship jolly good fun.

GLENN C. ALTSCHULER and JAN M. SALTZGABER

Ithaca, New York

PART ONE

For the Salvation of the World! Revivalism and Reform in Seneca Falls, New York

JAN M. SALTZGABER

The first sabbath in October 1843 was a busy one for the acting pastor of the Presbyterian Church of Seneca Falls. After the initial service of the day, he met with his elders to vote a resolution condemning slavery in America. At the second service, the resolve was presented to the congregation and unanimously accepted for distribution within the village and throughout the state. Immediately after the service, having publicly established their sentiments regarding slavery, the leaders of the church met again. This time, their purpose was to lay charges of "unchristian conduct" against Mrs. Rhoda Bement, one of the community's most fervent abolitionists. Behind this seemingly inconsistent series of events and the subsequent trial of Rhoda Bement lies a clash of principles which, in microcosm, reflects much of the tension in nineteenth-century American religion.

Eighteen forty-three, the year of the trial, was crucial to the village of Seneca Falls. The economy was changing and the village was on the cusp of a trend that altered its social complexion. New social and ethnic groups were entering the population and the community was stirred by demands for reform and political change. In this, Seneca Falls was not untypical of other rural western New York villages. Boosterism conflicted with the desire for a stable, orderly society; economic expansion was an obstacle to moral consensus. People sensed the power of voluntary association, the ability of common men and women to effect change, and many of them sought to unfetter human potentials by breaking with the past. Constraints on individual potential were variously perceived—the burden of sin and the unredeemed soul, slavery and the arrogance of southern planters, rum and the unconscionable profits of the liquor traffic, and even the smothering traditions of a patriarchal society. For many, it was sufficient to work to transform society by individual example and persuasion; more coercive methods threatened disruption. Others were more zealous. Impatient with the glacial pace of individual conversion, they embraced measures designed to hasten the perfection of America's promise.

Abigail (Abby) Kelley was one such zealot and she enlivened the late summer in Seneca Falls by delivering a series of abolition lectures. A former Quakeress, she had come to distrust organized religion as a result of her career in the antislavery movement. Too vehement to tolerate the gradualism and restraint of religious authorities, she combined abolitionism with a radical anticlericalism and candid attacks on the religious "establishment."[1] The very fact that Kelley took to the public podium and presumed to lecture "mixed" audiences on the immorality of slavery and the moral laxity of some clergy made her, by implication, a symbol of women's rights. Kelley's presence in Seneca Falls created an excitement that embroiled Rhoda Bement in conflict with her minister and ultimately with the government of her church.

Although Abby Kelley vilified the acting pastor of the Presbyterian Church, the Reverend Horace P. Bogue, as one who wanted to see abolitionists "burn," the minister chose not to respond in kind. He drew the line, however, at dignifying sim-

[1]See, e.g., Keith E. Melder, "Abigail Kelley Foster," *Notable American Women 1607–1950: A Biographical Dictionary*, vol. I, Edward T. James, Janet W. James, and Paul S. Boyer, eds. (Cambridge, Mass., 1971), pp. 647–650, and Gerda Lerner, *The Grimké Sisters from South Carolina: Pioneers for Women's Rights and Abolition* (Boston, 1971), p. 246.

ilar abolition meetings by announcing them from the pulpit. By handing up an announcement of a meeting for the last Sunday in September, Rhoda Bement tried to force Bogue to take a stand. To announce such a meeting was tantamount to an endorsement of abolition. To refuse was to tacitly acknowledge the justice of Kelley's accusation. Bogue sought to avoid the issue by claiming ignorance of the note, but clearly Mrs. Bement perceived his failure as a deliberate snub to ardent abolitionists within the church. When a second announcement went unread the following Sunday, she accused Bogue of duplicity. No longer a private matter, her open challenge to ministerial authority caused Bogue to convene the church session and have Bement charged with unchristian behavior, slander, and contempt for the discipline of the church. Although the minister and elders were willing to denounce slavery, they were not yet ready to endorse abolition, and they refused to countenance the acts of a zealot who threatened to push church policy beyond the community's own consensus.

The testimony in the ensuing trial of Rhoda Bement contains a wealth of evidence on the mores and attitudes of the people of Seneca Falls. It provides insights into the ethos of evangelism and reform in antebellum America. On the one hand, there was the determination of Americans to grow and expand, to escape the restrictive traditions of the past. On the other hand, in a new land subject to the constant influx of new peoples, communities—often created *de novo*—felt a pressing need for social order. Stability, however, often constrained progress. Predictability demanded institutional continuity, but such continuity tied people to their past. The transcript illuminates the conflict of centrifugal and centripetal forces, the struggle between people who looked for both an expansive future and a dependable present.

Such tension is a thread that runs throughout the record of the trial, revealing itself in four ways. First, one sees the yearning to liberate the individual from the bonds of Calvinist theology, which denied human volition. This desire is reflected in revival enthusiasm and the relationship between local churches and the community-at-large. Evangelical enthusiasm excited some church leaders' fears that fervor, if unchecked, might negate discipline and good order. Second, there is the concern for the emancipation of blacks from slavery and of whites from a domineering "slave power." Antislavery was viewed as a necessary step in the march toward the millennium, yet to press for an immediate and forcible interference with the "peculiar institution" could divide communities and undermine the influence of cautious leaders. Third, there is the temperance movement with its ardent expectation that freeing men from addiction to rum is tantamount to freeing society from sin. But whiskey and rum were also major items of commerce and, moreover, to move from moral suasion to forcible interference with business was to violate hallowed notions of individual freedom. Finally, there is the fact that Rhoda Bement was a woman challenging the thoroughly masculine power structure of her church. However unarticulated or unconscious her acts, she stood for the right of women to be heard publicly, and thus ran athwart one of the strongest traditions of nineteenth-century society. Her actions expressed the ideal of liberation from the "trammels of the past" but conflicted with an entrenched longing for the security that the familiar imparts. Her trial illustrates the stress within both her village and her country.

1

Change and the reluctance to change were part of the context of village life in Seneca Falls in the year of Rhoda Bement's trial. In the mid-forties the village of early settlement and growth was disappearing, and in its place one detects a community of maturing enterprises and more demanding competition. Though these social and economic changes are not referred to directly in the trial, they are the stage setting in which the drama is acted out.

The men and women dealt with in this work were, perhaps, more affected by social and economic change than most people in the community. The *dramatis personae* of the Bement trial represent only a limited part of the village social spectrum. They are not, by and large, members of the shifting substratum of hired workers and incidental laborers who are often beyond the reach of historical study. They form another milieu, the relatively prosperous professional and entrepreneurial class. They have significant ties to the community and a sense of village identity frequently expressed through a commitment to public service.[2] Affiliation with the Presbyterian or other churches, in itself, places them in a minority of village residents, albeit a large and influential minority. Although they were, in a sense, members of an elite, they were not insulated from the pressures of change but were, perhaps, even more sensitive to them than less committed villagers.

Community leaders, of course, saw Seneca Falls as uniquely

[2]The local records of Seneca Falls and Seneca County indicate that certain families and individuals constituted a village "elite" and were prone to assume leadership of the community and a variety of civic and social responsibilities. To cite a single name from a single source, *The Supervisors' Book for Seneca County,* Jonathan Metcalf appears over and over between 1826 and 1843 as: constable, justice of the peace, town clerk, inspector of elections, supervisor, coroner, inspector of schools, tax assessor, etc. In addition, his brothers, Joseph and Willard, also figure prominently in the county records. Jonathan Metcalf was also active as a church member, first in the Baptist and later in the Methodist Church, as well as in a host of other community services. He illustrates the nature of local leadership, combining civic and community service with active participation in Seneca Falls's Protestant churches. It seems clear from the examination of church records, local government sources, and other materials that community leadership correlates closely with Protestant church affiliation. Examination of the *Minutes of the* [Seneca Falls] *Village Board of Trustees* and church membership records clearly establishes that almost all the village leaders were active members of the Protestant churches. Of the twenty-six men who served as trustees between 1840 and 1843, six were Presbyterians, nine Episcopalians, two Methodists, and five were Baptists. Only four of the twenty-six cannot be definitively linked to one or another of the local churches. The records of the Episcopal Church in Seneca Falls are incomplete and it is quite possible that one or more of these four was an Episcopalian.

promising and aspired to raise the village to the dignity of a city. Yet their village was not exceptional and had much in common with other towns and villages of western New York including Geneva, Canandaigua, Lyons, and the arch rival, Waterloo.[3] Though Seneca Falls's economy rode out the depression of 1837 and villagers anticipated continued prosperity, the mood had changed. The first thirty years of the century had encouraged a sort of bouyant optimism based upon abundant waterpower and milling. Following the depression, however, the village was in transition and the 1840s saw the emergence of manufacturing and a new, less ebullient entrepreneurial spirit. Unfamiliar faces appeared in the streets while newer men assumed the mantle of economic leadership.

The career of Jeremy Bement, husband of the protagonist of our trial, illustrates the village's transition during the late 1830s and 1840s. It may be—one can only speculate—that the Bements' confrontation with religious authority in part reflected their own inner tensions and insecurity. Bement had arrived in Seneca Falls in the 1820s while the village was still in its first burst of economic growth. He entered into partnership with Abraham Buckout in 1829 to erect a substantial structure, the "Old Stone Shop," as a carriage factory. Their business flourished for some eight years until the 1837 Panic undercut the demand for wagons and carriages. Faced with hard times, Bement's affairs languished and, after a decade of relative success, he and his partner were forced to give up their shop. Bement was criticized for unscrupulous business practices by members of his own church and others, but never brought to court or indicted; his questionable ethics may have reflected a growing struggle for economic survival. He managed to remain in business on a diminished scale but, by the end of the decade, the economic climate of Seneca Falls was even less favorable and Bement's financial affairs were precarious. In 1849 he and

[3]Undated petition to New York State Legislature (ca. 1831) for the establishment of a bank in Seneca Falls, *Seneca Falls Historical Society Papers; Occasional Papers of the Seneca Falls Historical Society*, 1906.

his wife left to seek greater opportunities in Michigan, but in
Buffalo, New York, he contracted the cholera and died. With
Jeremy's death, the historian loses track of the Bement family.[4]

It may be that Bement's waning fortunes reflected the village's decreasing reliance on the processing of local agricultural
products and the consequent decline in the need for wagons.
In any event, Bement and Buckout's former carriage works was
purchased for a more industrial purpose; the "Old Stone Shop"
was turned into a pump factory. The initial effort failed, but
then Abel Downs, who owned the local cotton factory, bought
the building. Forming a partnership, he too undertook the
manufacture of pumps. Downs installed the first steam engine
in Seneca Falls and soon turned from the making of simple
wooden pumps to the production of modern iron designs. In
1852, Downs and his partners were bought out by Seabury S.
Gould. Expanding the facilities, Gould introduced large-scale
industrial organization and distributed his output throughout
the United States. Industrial methods, expanded capital investment, and an enlarged work force, then, symbolized the changes
in Seneca Falls. Many older mills were sold and converted to
industrial uses during the 1840s, and pioneer developers gave
way to a new generation of entrepreneurs.[5]

The transformation of the village economy was complete by
mid-century. Manufacturing replaced milling as the principle
occupation. Processing agricultural products remained important but was no longer the leading enterprise. During the first
half of the 1840s, in fact, two more flour mills were built and
Seneca Falls's daily output rose to some two thousand barrels,
but the balance was tipping and in the second half of the decade manufacturing clearly prevailed. An altered economy also
remolded village society. New jobs were generated and a different sort of worker attracted to the community. The social

[4]See the *Early Handwritten Credit Reporting Ledgers of the Mercantile Agency*, vol.
571, Baker Library, Harvard Business School, reports on July 25, 1845, February 22, 1847, March 23, 1849; see also records of the Seneca County Courts.
[5]H. Chamberlain, "Five Pivotal Years of Our History," *Occasional Papers of the
Seneca Falls Historical Society*, 1908, pp. 19–25.

order became more fixed as the economy matured and relationships between workers and their employers were formalized. Increasingly, individuals rejected voluntary participation in civic institutions and turned to the pursuit of private interest.[6] It must have seemed quite a different world to those who had helped to found the village and had shared in its early growth.

Significant as the 1840s were to Seneca Falls, some understanding of the earlier evolution from pioneer settlement to village and the nature of those who contributed to that evolution makes the transition clearer and helps to account for the stresses imposed on the community. The *personae* of the trial include many names that figured prominently in the early growth of Seneca Falls: Sackett, Bascom, King, McAlister, Lum, Bellows, Forman, and Matthews, among others. The falls of the Seneca River a mile or so from the western shore of Cayuga Lake had already attracted a scattering of settlers by 1790, but these pioneers were no match for the sophisticated men of business who soon turned a speculative eye on western lands. One such group toured western New York State with Elkanah Watson and reached the falls in September 1791. Quick to perceive the site's advantages, they formed a land development company under the direction of Stephen N. Bayard. Outbidding a local settler, Bayard and Company purchased the first of a series of lots that, between 1794 and 1816, gave them some fifteen hundred acres of land and exclusive control of water rights along the falls. Wilhelmus Mynderse, a company stockholder, was its resident agent and superintended erection of the first flour mill and other enterprises. Despite the enthu-

[6]The growing institutionalization of earlier voluntary activities is perhaps best seen in the *Minutes of the Board of Trustees of Seneca Falls*, in which the fire department is transformed from a purely voluntary organization whose membership was viewed both as obligation and honor to one which increasingly was forced to rely on paid members drawn from the less affluent and prominent elements of village society. For evidence of privatism in Utica and Rochester, see Paul E. Johnson, *A Shopkeeper's Millennium: Society and Revivals in Rochester, New York 1815–1837* (New York, 1978), pp. 15–36, and Mary P. Ryan, *Cradle of the Middle Class: The Family in Oneida County, New York, 1790–1865* (Cambridge, England, 1981), pp. 146ff.

siasm of its agent, the Bayard Company was essentially speculative and looked more to the appreciation of its investment than
to actual development. Unwilling to relinquish its monopoly yet
too distracted by other schemes, the company effectively stifled
growth for some thirty years.

Two events unlocked the settlement's future. Between 1825
and 1827, stockholders of Bayard and Company faced a series
of financial reverses and agreed to sell their holdings. For the
first time, the river's waterpower potential was opened to individual private development. The second stimulant was the link-
age of the Seneca River to the Erie Canal system. Incorporated
in 1813, the Seneca Lock Company controlled navigation along
the river. It completed navigational improvements in 1816 but
kept exclusive ownership for another eleven years. Then, in
1827, the state of New York took over the locks, enlarged and
improved the facilities, and joined the Seneca-Cayuga Canal
with the Erie. Canal improvements further enhanced "Seneca
Village" waterpower resources, set the stage for five years of
economic opportunity, and excited dreams of future greatness.[7]

Before the Bayard Company's demise, the locality was valued
for its agriculture. In a mildly optimistic mood, a settler's wife
wrote a friend in Connecticut: "I am much more reconciled to
the country than at first [her husband was hampered by a
drought] . . . but that must not hinder your coming here, it
may be better in the future. I think if you should come here
you would like the country for it is level and handsome . . . we
have the best kind of wheat here, and cider and apples enough
to be comfortable and all other kinds of fruit . . . very unsteady
weather but not much snow."[8] Men who came to be farmers or
purveyors soon began to see that Seneca Falls could be more
than a market center for local crops, that it presented opportunities for manufacturing and commerce to rival Rochester

[7]L. S. Sanford, "Early Industries," *Occasional Papers of the Seneca Falls Historical Society*, 1902, pp. 35–50.
[8]Hannah Beach to Mrs. Rachel Warner (Fairfield, Conn.), February 26, 1818, Seneca Falls Historical Society MSS.

and Syracuse. Seneca Falls was originally part of Junius Township, but by 1829 the natural advantages of the site coupled with the end of the Bayard monopoly attracted a sufficient population to warrant a separate township and, two years later, incorporation as Seneca Falls Village. Deficiencies in the original charter, however, forced reincorporation in 1837. Ansel Bascom, who was one of the early developers of the village, became its first president.

Chauncey Marshall, another leading developer as well as mill owner, voiced the general sense of enthusiasm for the village: "Population of 1500 . . . a large cotton factory that will go into operation in the spring (capital $100,000), a paper mill, a large distillery . . . [numerous other manufacturing and commercial ventures] . . . and our village rapidly increasing in every respect, and no village in the western part of the country (besides Rochester and Buffalo) will probably in a few years be equal to it."[9]

Five years after the demise of the Bayard monopoly, the population of Seneca Falls had doubled and the volume of business had increased threefold. Eighteen thirty-one saw the river lined with mills. Though flour milling was the primary enterprise, it now competed for waterpower with cotton, paper, and saw mills, not to mention the whiskey distilleries. A local newspaper, the *Seneca Farmer and Seneca Falls Advertiser,* published a letter from a "citizen" who listed an impressive inventory of enterprises:

1	Large Cotton Factory	17	Dry Good Stores
1	Small Woolen Factory	2	Hardwear Stores
5	Flouring Mills	2	Druggist Stores
1	Paper Mill	2	Shoe Stores
1	Large Tannery	2	Hat Stores
1	Large Distillery	3	Tin & Sheet Iron Factories
1	Sash Factory	1	Lead Pipe Factory beside
1	Furnace		many MFG est. & shops

[9]Chauncey Marshall to N. J. Benton, January 14, 1831, Seneca Falls Historical Society MSS.

24

1 Trip Hammer	5 Places of worship, 5 schools
5 Saw Mills	# of inhabitants 1,800–2,000[10]
1 Carriage Factory	

The citizen neglected to include the potash factory, several brick-yards, blacksmiths, doctors, lawyers, livery stables, and a host of groceries, taverns, and hotels. The pace of expansion continued throughout the 1830s until checked by the Panic at the end of the decade.

If some men like Jeremy Bement felt the depression rather sharply, others did not. The tinsmith Joseph Corl seemed little affected by local hard times. Though moved to diversify his investments by speculating in Michigan lands, he wrote to a business associate:

> Crops, except wheat which is pretty good, are very fine—business, so so—times seem hard—tho' not half as much as they are cried up to be—improvement in our village progressing moderately—so that on the whole we are not so bad off as we might be, or as many other places are said to be—besides all seem to have hope, as they may well have . . . I have no doubt that the year will close upon us again a prosperous & improving people—all the croakers to the contrary not withstanding.[11]

Not everyone, of course, was quite so sanguine as Corl. In 1840 a small merchant named E. J. Davis admonished his customers to pay up their accounts in an advertisement with the headline "The times are hard up and so am I." Still, in the same year the *Seneca Falls Democrat* smugly reflected that, "while she [Seneca Falls] did not grow as some of her sister villages during the speculating era, she does not drop like them during the pressure."[12] And two years later, possibly whistling in the dark,

[10]*Seneca Farmer and Seneca Falls Advertiser*, August 15, 1832, Seneca Falls Historical Society Newspaper Collection.
[11]Joseph Corl to Seba Murphey, July 25, 1837, Seneca Falls Historical Society MSS.
[12]*Seneca Falls Democrat*, August 13, 1840, and December 3, 1840, Seneca Falls Historical Society Newspaper Collection.

the *Democrat* added: "Notwithstanding the hard times, the village is going ahead, as the phrase is, like a Steam Boat. New buildings are going up in every quarter, and the old ones are being refitted. Most of our mills, and other large manufacturing establishments, are in full operation; and our merchants are selling goods by the wholesale—no wonder though, considering the prices they sell at."[13] In fact, the village was going ahead, if not like a "Steam Boat," then with all deliberate speed. And, if the growing number of mill hands and other new workers disturbed an earlier harmony, many merchants were doing a good business.

The decade of growth from 1827 to 1837 reflected the energies of men who combined private speculation and self-interest with public-spiritedness. Three men figure most prominently in the burgeoning of the early village: Gary Van Sackett, Ansel Bascom, and Andrew Tillman. These three, along with lesser investors, purchased large tracts of the Bayard Company's land. Although they acted in their own interests and hoped to benefit from a general mood of optimism, they were not mere opportunists. Each was committed to the welfare of the community-as-a-whole. Retaining a portion of their land for private use, they subdivided the remainder and offered it to the public at comparatively low prices and on exceptionally easy terms.[14] If such men saw expanding enterprise as a means of capitalizing on their own large acreages, they were more than real-estate speculators. They were entrepreneurs surely, but they were involved in the life of the village through a strong sense of personal dedication and moral obligation. They were builders in the best sense of the word.

Gary V. Sackett illustrates the type. Born in Vermont, he came west to share the region's growth and progress. He first settled in the village of Cayuga on the east side of the lake where he practiced law, but then moved to Bridgeport, located where the Seneca River joins the lake, and in 1814 Sackett

[13]Ibid., June 9, 1842.
[14]*Occasional Papers of the Seneca Falls Historical Society*, 1908, passim.

established a homestead about a mile up the river at the future site of Seneca Falls. In partnership with Luther F. Stevens, he conducted a joint practice of law until 1823, when both he and Stevens were appointed to judgeships. Concerned with almost every facet of public life, Sackett corresponded with leading figures in state and national government, including William Seward, Millard Fillmore, and Thurlow Weed. A proud "amateur" farmer deeply engrossed by experimental agriculture, he became the first president of the Seneca County Agriculture Society. Sackett's varied interests reflected his desire for a prosperous and stable village, a community certainly sparked by economic growth yet integrated by willing cooperation and orderliness.[15]

Sackett, who was a vestryman of Trinity Episcopal Church, was convinced that the village's churches were a stabilizing influence and, as such, a crucial element of community. As with others, his own denominational loyalties were no barrier to general benevolence. In an age of prejudice toward "Papism," he freely contributed land for a Roman Catholic Church. If there were to be a Roman Catholic population within the village, Sackett felt the social and moral benefits of church membership would make the Catholics more secure and their presence less unsettling to the community. As Mynderse donated land for the Methodist Episcopal Church, though not himself a Methodist, so Sackett and other landowners felt a debt to the spiritual as well as the material well-being of the community.[16]

Such men, of course, were highly pragmatic and recognized that there could be no community without a firm economic foundation. Sackett joined with Mynderse and others in building "Mechanic's Hall," a commercial block intended to help develop the south side of the Seneca River. Rivalry between the two banks of the river was fairly marked. The northern shore was older and better developed, but Sackett successfully cham-

---

[15]*Occasional Papers of the Seneca Falls Historical Society*, 1903, 1905, 1908, passim.

[16]*Occasional Papers of the Seneca Falls Historical Society*, 1905, passim, and *History of Seneca County, New York* (Philadelphia, 1876), pp. 113, 114.

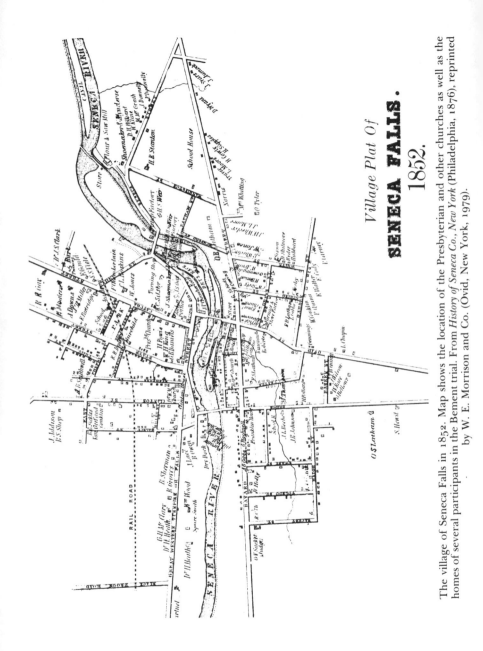

Village Plat Of
SENECA FALLS.
1852.

The village of Seneca Falls in 1852. Map shows the location of the Presbyterian and other churches as well as the homes of several participants in the Bement trial. From *History of Seneca Co., New York* (Philadelphia, 1876), reprinted by W. E. Morrison and Co. (Ovid, New York, 1979).

pioned the south side of the river where he held land. Commercial competition was paralleled by the political contention between the First Ward on the north and the Second on the south. Political antagonism revolved around questions of taxation and municipal improvements and, like economic wrangling, was part of the village's growing pains.

Despite communal squabbles, growth was the chief aim. When the Bayard Company announced the pending sale of its land and water rights, Sackett built a distillery and oil and grist mills, all of which he then sold to a promising newcomer. A year later he and Chauncey Marshall constructed a paper mill to process the abundant local softwoods. Again, Sackett turned active operation of the mill over to others. Apparently, he saw himself as a promoter of enterprise, a man who encouraged others to step in to amplify the village economy.[17]

Seneca Falls's boosters, like their counterparts in other nineteenth-century American communities, faced an almost insurmountable task.[18] They reckoned on the need for continuity and village harmony at the same time that they confronted a significant turnover in population. Faith in laissez-faire capitalism and the hope for economic expansion vied with the equally

[17]See passim, *Sackett Family Papers*, Seneca Falls Historical Society; Biographical Sketches in *Occasional Papers of the Seneca Falls Historical Society*, 1903; and Edward C. Eisenhart, *A Century of Seneca Falls History—Showing the Rise and Progress of a New York State Village* (unpublished A.B. thesis, Princeton University, 1942).
[18]Histories of community are largely dominated by attempts to identify the decay of an earlier cultural, religious, and ethnic homogeneity. In a recent work Thomas Bender seeks to avoid "being trapped by the logic of collapse" and exhorts historians to examine the persistence of community. Whether they champion breakdown or persistence, we believe, historians have ignored an important fact in American history: for two and a half centuries following the settlement of Jamestown and Boston, Americans continued to *create* communities where none existed before. This task of creation was complicated by an overwhelming amount of transiency. The evidence of the records of Seneca Falls tends to support Michael Katz's argument that "transiency forms the first great theme of a nineteenth-century city" and that the search for "a satisfactory way of interrelating structural rigidity and personal transiency" is the "central intellectual task for the students of past societies." See, Michael B. Katz, *The People of Hamilton, Canada West: Family and Class in a Mid-Nineteenth-Century-City* (Cambridge, Mass., 1976), p. 38.

worthy hope for communal stability. A stable community was vital since economic interaction in the antebellum era relied largely upon trust; ready cash was notoriously short and business operated chiefly on credit, with promissory notes based on a verbal assurance of credit-worthiness routinely substituting for money.[19] Verification was difficult and belief in the honesty of a man's word was fundamental to economic security. Still, businessmen could hardly limit sales to personal acquaintances. Economic survival itself compelled merchants to risk dealing with strangers.

While "communities"—aggregates of people who identified with the village and had intimate knowledge of one another's character and background through multiple associations and institutional affiliations—undoubtedly existed in Seneca Falls, community in the broader sense proved elusive. Ultimately, it was impossible to create an environment of predictability, security, and stability which embraced the vast majority of people. Profit seeking and expansion guaranteed the continual ebb and flow of major segments of the population. Located on a vital branch of the Erie Canal system and, after 1841, of the railroad, Seneca Falls was especially prone to transiency. Native-born Americans and immigrants searching for work were a source of cheap labor and a ready market for the town's merchants. They were also a source of paupers, criminals, and heathens.[20]

New enterprises attracted new peoples who came not to farm but to labor in mills and stores. The canal and other internal improvements pulled many restless folk from New England and the Middle Atlantic states westward, but many of the newcomers were foreigners: Canadian, German, English, French,

[19]The most revealing evidence of this characteristic of nineteenth-century commerce is in the records of the Seneca County courts. The amount of litigation regarding default of payment and, more illuminating, the severity with which financial crime was treated relative to crimes of violence suggest an almost insurmountable challenge to the business community. See records of County and Justice Courts, Seneca County Courthouse, Waterloo, New York.

[20]See Glenn Altschuler and Jan Saltzgaber, "Clearinghouse for Paupers: The Seneca County Poorfarm, 1830–1860" (unpublished MS).

and Irish. Alien religious doctrines and a highly visible minority of outsiders may have exacerbated social tensions.[21] A heightened social polarization replaced the sense of easy social mobility that had characterized the early stages of settlement in Seneca Falls. The socioeconomic lines hardened with the coming of the French-Canadian mill hand or the Irish "canawler."

Antebellum western New York was less and less insulated from the events and forces that influenced the nation. With the passing of the New York frontier, the rural population was no longer preoccupied with mere survival. Land pressure promoted generational conflicts and found expression in religious and social turmoil. The original agricultural base was surpassed as economic growth took the form of commercial and industrial development. The canal, the railroads, the postal system, and the development of the popular press all helped to break down the relative isolation of upstate communities. Future cities such as Rochester, Utica, and Syracuse and even smaller localities such as Seneca Falls were, in some degree, hostage to the business cycles of the national economy. The interchange between newer and older centers reflected not only the flow of goods but also the communication of ideas and enthusiasms.

The village of Seneca Falls shared with the rest of the nation the boom of the 1820s and 1830s and the depression of the 1840s. Its early growth excited village boosters with images of large-scale prosperity; the changes following the Panic of 1837 introduced a less certain era, one that for many produced a sense of impending revolution. The changes witnessed by the people of western New York often seemed literally earthshaking; to some it appeared the millennium was at hand.[22] It seems

[21]For general treatments of this phenomenon see Joel H. Silbey, *The Transformation of American Politics, 1840–1860* (Englewood Cliffs, N.J., 1967), and Ronald Formisano, *The Birth of Mass Political Parties, Michigan, 1827–1861* (Princeton, N.J., 1971).

[22]See e.g., D. T. Arthur, "Millerism," in *The Rise of Adventism*, ed. Edwin S. Gaustad (New York, 1974). The classic treatment of millennial thought in America remains Ernest Lee Tuveson, *Redeemer Nation: The Idea of America's Millennial Role* (Chicago, 1968). See also, Winthrop S. Hudson, *American Protestantism* (Chicago, 1961), and William McLoughlin, *Revivals, Awakenings, and Reform* (Chicago, 1978).

evident that the economy of Seneca Falls, and of the broader region as well, significantly affected religious attitudes. Whitney Cross, historian of the Burned-Over District, argues that people were most receptive to the appeal of religious enthusiasm during the "post-fever" phase of the economy, when the frantic boom of the canal era was replaced by less frenzied and more modest prosperity. In boom times they were too busy trying to make money and, in times of bust, they were preoccupied with trying to keep it.[23] Such may have been the case in the village of Seneca Falls when, as we have seen, the depression of the 1840s, although not wrecking the prosperity of the community, slowed the pace of development, transformed the character of enterprise, and tempered optimism with caution. The generation after the opening of the Erie Canal spawned a host of religious, social, and political movements—Mormonism, Spiritualism, Millerism, perfectionist societies, Anti-Masonry, the Liberty and Free-Soil parties among many others—all in the region that the revivalist Charles Grandison Finney described as "burned-over."

2

The excitements of religious fervor—as well as of abolitionism, the temperance movement, and the demand for women's rights—were played out against this backdrop of tension bred by the coincident desires for change and stability. Religious enthusiasm played a central role in the formation of nineteenth-century community, and historians have used two models to explain its function in the antebellum ethos. One model stresses unity as the motivating force that initiated revivalism; the other pictures revivalism as divisive in its consequences, splitting both the Protestant religious community and the larger social body.

[23]Whitney R. Cross, *The Burned-Over District, The Social and Intellectual History of Enthusiastic Religion in Western New York 1800–1850* (Ithaca, 1950) pp. 55ff.

Since revival broadened the membership of churches, it was welcomed by ministers and lay leaders who perceived an opportunity for extending their influence in the community. Yet revival could be a two-edged sword since it stressed the individual will and deemphasized the authority of the trained ministry. With his or her impatience for change, the enthusiast often encountered resistance from those concerned with the continuity of institutional structures. Spiritual ardor needed limits if it were to be harnessed in the service of the church and community.

Not surprisingly, the churches of Seneca Falls were recognized as bulwarks of social stability. Church members commonly felt themselves beleaguered by hosts of the ungodly.[24] Threatened, as we have seen, by new elements in its midst, an anxious population may have translated its insecurities into appeals to emotionalism and calls for social activism. While attempting to extend the churches' moral discipline over the whole community, those within the fold must present a united front. A church could interpret open dissent only as a weakening of the fragile fabric of community.

Josiah T. Miller, a prominent lawyer and the editor of the *Seneca Falls Democrat,* reflected the sentiment of community leaders when he wrote in the first issue of the paper that it was better to attend any church than none at all. All major denominations were represented in Seneca Falls, where the churches had been among the first institutions established. They shared in the general current of religious enthusiasm which "burnt" western New York in the 1830s and 1840s and were vulnerable to the reforms that revivalism spawned. Protestant church membership certainly numbered no more than a quarter of the total village populace and possibly less. Nevertheless, with few exceptions, the economic and social leaders of the village were

[24]The records of the Seneca Falls Baptist, Methodist, and Presbyterian Churches in the Department of Manuscripts and University Archives, Cornell University, Ithaca, N.Y. (hereafter cited as M and UA, CU), along with the records of other churches in western New York, are a rich source of attitudes toward the church and the community.

33

affiliated with one or another of the churches. Denominational loyalties and doctrinal rivalries were muted. Preference dictated church membership, but the chief thing for Seneca Falls's elite was their identification with the discipline of organized religion.

The Presbyterian church was the first to be established within the community and its history is fairly typical. It had begun as a pioneer association among New Englanders who settled along the river. Founded in 1807, it predated both the township and village of Seneca Falls. The "First Presbyterian Church of Junius" initially met in a barn and did not have a real church until 1812. Following the dictates of the Plan of Union,[25] the church included both Presbyterians and Congregationalists. The combination of two variants of Calvinist doctrine apparently generated some tension, however, and in 1833 some three dozen members withdrew to form a separate Congregational Church. Among those who broke away were the brother of Rhoda Bement, Elias Denison, and the physician-druggist Dr. Joseph K. Brown. Apparently, the secession did not involve serious rancor and when it proved impossible to sustain the new church, most members returned to the Presbyterian fold.[26]

The mood set by a church's individual pastors and its lay authorities often determined sectarian loyalty and the choice of denomination. When groups of communicants or specific individuals did withdraw from a particular church, it was usually in reaction to an unpopular preacher. Rhoda Bement is one case in point. Prior to her membership in the Presbyterian Church, she had been affiliated with the Baptists. Evidently

[25]After a period of informal alliance, Congregational and Presbyterian churches formed a nationwide cooperative agreement in 1801 between the Presbyterian Church of the Middle States and the Congregrationalists of New England. Inspired by evangelical zeal, the Plan of Union gave formal sanction to the existing practice of ministers of the two denominations to cooperate in founding churches in the regions of new settlement, especially New York State. Authority was divided along the New England–New York line with new churches in the East joining the Congregational Associations and those of the West affiliated with the Presbyterian Synods. See, e.g., George M. Marsden, *The Evangelical Mind and the New School Presbyterian Experience* (New Haven, Conn., 1970), pp. 10ff, and Cross, *The Burned-Over District*, pp. 18–19.
[26]*History of Seneca County*, pp. 113–114.

finding it impossible to reconcile her convictions with the views of the local church, she left the Baptists and joined the Presbyterians. Subsequent to her confrontation with the Reverend Horace Bogue and the Session of the Presbyterian Church, she joined the Wesleyan Methodists, whose position on slavery was closer to her own.[27] Group defections were rarer and sometimes led by a charismatic minister. In 1843, the beleaguered Baptist Church was split when a Millerite preacher formed a small, independent Adventist Church around Baptist dissidents.[28] But disaffection, individual or group, almost never alienated the dissenters from organized religion per se.

Seneca Falls was located on the "psychic highway" in the core region of the Second Great Awakening. Whitney Cross, in his history of the Burned Over District, identified two major zones of religious enthusiasm. One arched northward from Madison County to encompass the thriving commercial-manufacturing towns of Rome and Utica. The second stretched southeastward from the burgeoning city of Rochester. Between these areas, revivals were a regular occurrence but their frequency and fervor was less intense. Roughly associated with the Erie Canal and its branches, the geography of revivalism is ill defined but the outburst of enthusiasm reverberated well beyond the most ardent centers. Its repercussions echoed throughout the antebellum era.[29]

Though perhaps more muted than in some other communities, revivalism played a prominent part in Seneca Falls's religious life. Revivals occurred throughout the 1830s and significantly widened church membership, especially among Baptists, Methodists, and Presbyterians. Extended prayer meetings and "special labors" gained sixty new members for the Baptist Church in 1837. Another sixty were harvested the following

[27]Session Minutes, First Presbyterian Church of Seneca Falls, November 15, 1844, M and UA, CU.

[28]Minutes, First Baptist Church of Seneca Falls, 1843, M and UA, CU.

[29]See generally, Cross, *The Burned-Over District*, pp. 277ff, and John L. Thomas, "Romantic Reform in America, 1815–1865," *American Quarterly* 17 (1965), pp. 656–681.

year. Membership in the church approached two hundred active communicants and the sabbath school registered over three hundred "scholars."[30] Since the church experienced considerable financial difficulty in the mid-thirties, these revivals may have reflected practical as well as spiritual concerns. Whatever the motive, Baptist membership expanded as a result of the skillful evangelism of local laymen and clergy. Nor did they neglect the help of outside luminaries. The Baptist preacher Joseph Knapp, whose fame rivaled that of the Presbyterian Charles Grandison Finney, conducted the 1838 revival with outstanding success.[31]

Although there is no specific mention of revival in the records of the Presbyterian Church, the congregation's growth in the 1830s suggests a spirit similar to that of the Baptists. Revivalism was frequently a two-stage process in which the battle for individual souls preceded a struggle for the soul of a depraved society.[32] Whether in the guise of abolitionism, the temperance movement, or the call for women's rights, reform captured the imagination of many, but not of all. Some of the devout, possibly even a majority, saw the churches as properly and exclusively concerned with individual conversion. For these men and women, social reform strained the bounds of righteousness and was an unwarranted provocation of community norms. The reforming zeal of Abby Kelley and her supporter Rhoda Bement posed a threat to the authority of those village and church leaders unprepared to endorse doctrines of social and political action. Clearly, men like Bogue were willing to pass resolutions that used passive example in an attempt to influence private convictions. Just as evident, however, was their unwillingness to countenance political actions that might separate from their church coreligionists who were indifferent to the evils of slavery. To embroil the church in questions of social

---

[30]Baptist Church Records of Seneca Falls, Sunday School Register, M and UA, CU.

[31]Baptist Church Records of Seneca Falls, 1838, M and UA, CU.

[32]See, e.g., Bernard A. Weisberger, *They Gathered at the River: The Story of the Great Revivalists and Their Impact upon Religion in America* (Boston, 1958), pp. 149, 152.

conscience was to imperil the unity of both church and community; those who insisted on active reform must either be shown the error of their ways or, as a last resort, be thrust from the church.

The tensions one detects in the Bement trial reflect not only the stresses within a changing community but also the broad context of religious disquiet in a society undergoing rapid social and economic change. Although well beyond the pioneer stage of development, the people of "the Falls" shared the image of America as a "new" world, an unspoiled environment that invited boundless hopes. It may have been easy to endow America with the mantle of the New Jerusalem and to see the nation as a potential Eden, yet, for all the expectancy, there was the haunting fear that Eden might too easily succumb to the vice of materialism. Somehow, America's promise was never quite fulfilled. In Seneca Falls, as in Eden, Christian humility often encountered self-satisfied pride. Aware that the ideal seldom matched the reality, many people were apprehensive about the battle between morality and selfishness and their insecurity was heightened by the rootlessness of their communities.

Uncertainties within nineteenth-century society often manifested themselves in religious emotionalism and the urge to act upon apparent contradictions. Revivalism emphasized the will of man and turned away, however hesitantly, from the bondage of Calvinist doctrine. Calvinism tied men to the notion of "election" and denied the capacity of the human will to effect change. Presbyterian and Congregational evangelists may have formally accepted the conservative, pessimistic insistence on man's corrupted nature; nevertheless, they held that moral depravity did not preclude man's freedom of will. If Calvinist theology placed man within the "trammels of inability," revivalism sought his liberation and responded not only to Calvinism but also to Universalism which held the love of God to be so all-inclusive that no man could avoid salvation. Neither doctrine recognized man's will as an instrument of salvation. Nor, by implication, did either of the doctrines perceive any ultimate worth in man's effort to ameliorate the human condition.

Nineteenth-century America, however, was ill suited to a doctrine of inability. The hazards of the natural and social environment put a premium on human volition and struggle. Revivalism effectively instilled a belief in the principle of voluntarism and focused the force of religious zeal on America's moral and social ills. Indeed, upstate New York has been described as, "the storm center, and religious forces were driving propellants of social movements important for the whole country in that generation."[33] The churches of Seneca Falls were not immune to that religious and social ferment.

Revivalism made people take an active part in their own salvation and whole communities engaged in organizing successful and stimulating religious campaigns.[34] Managing events leading to salvation was a heady experience and the zealot who felt "reborn" could hardly relapse into spiritual passivity. But salvation necessarily awaits the end of one's life; in the meantime, what was to be done? Spiritual enthusiasm led many faithful to embrace social activism as a means of bringing about change. Though still concerned with organizational and doctrinal formalities as necessary to guide and promote change, religious zealots made action the highest priority. Many people adopted the post-millennial view that the thousand-year earthly reign of Christ had already begun. And, if the new age were at hand, it imposed an obligation to militant perfectionism—a commitment extending beyond individual salvation to the reform and perfection of the whole of society. Recognizing that society was compounded of good and evil, reformers demanded that men and women manifest their moral potential by acting to suppress sin. In short, such reformers perceived society as both promise and threat; they were convinced that man could obviate the threat by his own volition.

Perhaps the most useful perception of antebellum revivalism

[33]Cross, *The Burned-Over District*, p. ix.

[34]See, e.g., Cross, *The Burned-Over District*, pp. 153ff; William McLoughlin, *Modern Revivalism: Charles Grandison Finney to Billy Graham* (New York, 1959), pp. 54ff; Weisberger, *They Gathered at the River*, pp. 106–107; and Johnson, *Shopkeeper's Millennium*, pp. 4ff and passim.

is as intellectual emancipation. Like the American Revolution, revivalism sought to liberate men, but like the Revolution it also posed the question how freedom ought to be used. Revivalism transposes religion from the passive to the active voice and in so doing notably extended the layman's role in the religious life of his community. Liberating religious thought and practice from the formalism of the past mirrored, and possibly promoted, the general trend toward self-help through voluntarism. Clergy who resisted the emotionalism of revivalism or reform were freely criticized. Lay men and women such as Mrs. Bement pressed for the abandonment of clerical prejudice or even, in some cases, the dismissal of the cleric. Bement's willingness to challenge the authority of her minister demonstrates the laity's increased confidence in its capacity for action. The prominence of the laity in church government and its domination of benevolent and reform societies harmonized with a religious ideology that stressed individual volition and, with America's growing voluntarism, expanded the influence of the common man and woman over the nation's religious and social life.[35]

3

The tendencies of revivalism—emotionalism, immediacy, and moral absolutism—were among the factors that inspired the movement for social reform in mid-nineteenth-century America. Like revivalism, reform juxtaposed an eagerness for change with a fear of disorder. The Bement trial is essentially focused on the discord between zealous reformers and cautious traditionalists. Two reforms were uppermost in the mind of Rhoda Bement, and each was a serious threat to the unity of her church. Abolition and temperance were equally concerned with freedom and neither could be achieved without violence to

[35]Weisberger, *They Gathered at the River*, pp. 85–86, and Cross, *The Burned-Over District*, pp. 45, 136, and passim.

existing values and conventions, without challenge to communal solidarity.

For the spiritual zealot-turned-reformer, the correction of society's ills was a logical extension of revivalism. The struggle for the individual soul was always subject to frustration so long as the larger society persisted in its sinful behavior. And to many, America seemed iniquitous indeed. It appeared that most men and women were indifferent to both the demands of salvation and the cry for social reform. In the activists' eyes, indifference to great social wrongs was as reprehensible as apathy toward a healthy soul. When Rhoda Bement confronted her minister with the accusation, "You told me you was an abolitionist & I supposed if you was you would read abolition notices,"[36] she was voicing her indignation at the halfhearted. The unconverted, the unconvinced, and even the lukewarm, those who rejected reform or gave only conditional support—all were sinners. They had to be won over, and the sooner the better. In nineteenth-century revivals, the conversion experience was compressed into a few hours, or at most a few days. Reformers, conditioned by the immediacy of spiritual rebirth, also sought their objectives now and at once, convinced that to do otherwise was to compromise with sin. At times the political process itself was denigrated as a perverse mechanism designed to maintain the status quo.[37] Many reformers were unwilling to brook delay on the road to the promised land.

[36]Many people who were dedicated to eradicating slavery were nevertheless cautious and inclined to see the solution in the removal of slaves to distant lands. Horace Bogue, an agent for the American Colonization Society in the 1840s, seems to have had this attitude. Abolitionists, who perceived slavery as an unredeemable sin that might bring about divine retribution, sought to end slavery immediately, and therefore viewed the American Colonization Society with suspicion. See David Brion Davis, "The Emergence of Immediatism in British and American Anti-Slavery Thought," in *Ante-Bellum Reform* (New York, 1967), ed. David Brion Davis, pp. 139–152. See also, James Brewer Stewart, *Holy Warriors: The Abolitionists and American Slavery* (New York, 1976); Merton L. Dillon, *Abolitionists: The Growth of a Dissenting Minority* (New York, 1979); Gerald Sorin, *The New York Abolitionist: A Case Study of Radicalism* (Westport, Conn., 1970); and Aileen Kraditor, *Means and Ends in American Abolitionism* (New York, 1967).

[37]See, e.g., Weisberger, *They Gathered at the River*, p. 155, and Henry Steele Commager, *The Era of Reform, 1830–1860* (Princeton, N.J., 1960), pp. 11–13.

Moral absolutism of this sort, sometimes labeled "Ultraism," had, by the 1840s, already generated schism within the nation's Protestant denominations.[38] Since no local church wanted to repeat these nationwide divisions within its own congregation, church regulations and formal disciplinary codes were all aimed at reconciliation. As the trial of Rhoda Bement illustrates, it was hoped that the fellowship of the church and its collective wisdom, embodied in the minister and the board of elders, would curb extremists. The churches valued consensus and, in any open confrontation with reformers, a church's first priority was to convince the dissident of his or her error. Only with great reluctance did the church resort to exclusion.

For many in Seneca Falls, Abby Kelley's lectures threatened to produce just such a confrontation. Her fervid stand against the evil of slavery was a marked contrast to the complacency or indifference of ordinary citizens and, seemingly, it had begun to change their thinking. When Thomas Van Alstyne was queried by the Session about his attitudes toward slavery, he indicated that he had previously accepted the institution as one supported by biblical and religious principles. At the same time, however, his statements indicate that, if not totally converted to abolitionism, he had at least begun to experience doubts about slavery's moral justifications. Even more serious was the testimony of Mrs. Perry, who, having attended her first lecture on abolition, found her thinking changed and was apparently convinced of the immorality of slavery. Her admission that she knew little of the issue before Kelley's lecture and that her ignorance was due to the church authorities, who "had never told us anything about it" but had left her to "suppose there was no very great sin in it," was a significant indictment of the minister and the elders. Where authorities were content to ignore the slavery issue, its intrusion upon the conscience of the congregation was a matter of considerable import and potential discord.[39]

[38]See, e.g., Cross, *The Burned-Over District,* pp. 198ff.
[39]See Part 2, p. 121.

For many ultraists the crusade against slavery provided a test of religious conviction. Abolition, while obviously a revolutionary social change, was couched in the terminology of revivalism. The slaveholder was indicted as a manstealer who exploited the labor of others. The indictment dwelt not on the inherent injustice and inequality of slavery—the social offense done to black men and women which belied the tenets of American democracy—but on the moral evil of idleness and the fact that the master earned his bread by another man's sweat. Southern plantation owners were far more likely to be pictured as exemplars of sin than as authors of social injustice. And by extension, the sin was shared by those who failed to commit themselves fully to the eradication of slavery. Thus, ultraists claimed that those who traded for southern goods or invested in the plantation economy were steeped in sin. The existence of slavery was a perpetual reminder of the unredeemed character of America, the acquiescence to a wrong that barred religious regeneration.

Northern abolitionism was by no means popular. Many people, particularly among the religious leadership, criticized abolitionists for the vehemence of their attacks upon those associated with slavery. Abolitionists were accused of substituting emotionalism for genuine religious and social conviction, of turning their enthusiasm against authority, and of denouncing otherwise virtuous and reputable Christians. In their single-minded devotion to the cause of abolition, zealots were censured for a lack of both dignity and regard for proper forms of action. Antislavery "fanatics" often seemed both powerful and uncontrolled, a part of the democratization of America in the 1820s and 1830s which some considered a threat to the power of a wise and temperate leadership. In the 1830s antislavery advocates in the North had been the targets of considerable violence, but the panic of 1837 and the ensuing depression eroded some of the resistance to abolition. The 1840s saw an intensification of local and regional insecurities, a process that sharpened sectional rivalries and exaggerated the image of the

For the Salvation of the World!

sinful southern aristocrat.[40] Moderation and compromise seemed even less acceptable to abolitionists and the press for immediate reform grew. Yet the southern slaveholder was not the only evil. More insidious and therefore more reprehensible were his northern confederates, those who were merely neutral on the slavery issue. The Reverend Horace P. Bogue apparently advocated a cautious approach to the slavery question. Bogue's ties with the American Colonization Society[41] stamp him as an antislavery gradualist who thought abolition yielded more heat than light. The minister accepted the importance of individual conversion but held back from translating religious enthusiasm into social action. To some of his flock, at least, Bogue's caution must have seemed timidity or even obstructionism. They had heard such stalwart antislavery workers as the Grimké sisters and their associate, Abby Kelley, argue that resettlement of blacks in Africa would aid slaveholders by relieving their embarrassment at the presence of free black men. Angelina Grimké wrote: "That the Colonization Society is a benevolent institution we deny . . . the

[40]See, e.g., Avery Craven, "The Northern Attack on Slavery," in *Ante-Bellum Reform*, pp. 22ff, and Leonard Richards, *Gentlemen of Property and Standing: Anti-Abolition Mobs in Jacksonian America* (New York, 1970), passim. See especially Donald M. Scott, *From Office to Profession: The New England Ministry, 1750–1850* (Camden, N.J., 1978), pp. 96–100. In quoting a 1836 letter from Charles G. Finney to Theodore Weld, Scott suggests something of the anxiety abolitionism provoked among some evangelical churchmen: "Br. Weld is it not true, at least do you not fear it is, that we are in our present course going fast into civil war? Will not our present movements in abolition result in that? Shall we not ere long be obliged to take refuge in a military depotism? Have you no fear of this? If not, why have you not? Nothing is more manifest to me than that the present movements will result in this, unless your mode of abolitionizing the country is greatly modified."

[41]The American Colonization Society was founded in 1816 for the purpose of promoting the voluntary resettlement of free Negroes in Africa. Initial leadership reflected the moderate and humane elements in the slave states— such men as Henry Clay or James Madison—and looked to the removal of large numbers of freedmen from the southern population. Though the society was not concerned with emancipation directly and certainly did not want it immediately, it did hope that colonization would lead slaveowners to free their bondsmen in order to send them out of the country. For more radical abolitionists, the society seemed intent only on removing free blacks and thus strengthening slavery as an institution.

43

free colored people are to be exiled, because public opinion is crushing them into the dust. . . . Surely you never want to 'get rid' of people whom you love."[42]

As intensely as the Grimké sisters felt about the plight of black men and women in America, abolition was a rather abstract notion to most people in western New York. Slavery was an institution of the remote South—well removed from the realities of their daily lives—and perhaps for that reason abolitionism was less dangerously divisive than other reform movements. Temperance, sabbatarianism, and even the reform of schools and prisons cut against certain community interests and might generate factionalism.[43] If local reforms were more immediate and divisive, it may have seemed easier to direct one's zeal against the distant southern slaveholder. For reformers stimulated by revivalism, the "peculiar institution" of the 1840s was the most satanic force in American society.

Change in the American economy and the consequent social pressures were other factors in the antislavery movement. Financial and industrial urban centers had expanded and urbanization in turn modified the nature of agriculture as enterprising farmers responded to these new and lucrative markets by adopting improved and specialized husbandry. Change never comes without cost. Many people were hard pressed to compete and found themselves isolated from the upward progress of economic development. Even industry failed in its promise when overexpansion led to the Panic of 1837. New Englanders, especially, found themselves dispossessed. Turning to the new land, they spawned a "greater New England" in western New York and the Great Lakes basin. But relocation involved a re-

---

[42]*Letters to Catherine E. Beecher* (Boston, 1838), pp. 35–36, 40, as quoted in Lerner, *The Grimké Sisters*, p. 185.

[43]See, e.g., Johnson, *Shopkeeper's Millennium*, pp. 74ff, in regard to the controversy over sabbatarianism; see also passim the Minutes of the Board of Trustees of the Village of Seneca Falls, especially in regard to temperance and licensing ordinances; also, Joseph Gusfield, *Symbolic Crusade: Status and the American Temperance Movement* (Urbana, Ill., 1963); Michael B. Katz, *The Irony of Early School Reform: Educational Innovation in Mid-Nineteenth Century Massachusetts* (Boston, 1970).

newed struggle for the establishment of security. Surpluses from the fields of Ohio and Illinois were a continual source of competition for those just beginning to realize some measure of prosperity. The "hard times" of the late 1830s and 1840s further encouraged a widened democracy among Americans. Resentment of special privilege was more sharply honed and the demand for the restoration of prosperity assumed a harsher note. New bastions of privilege such as the southern plantation owners and their allies, the millowners and great merchants, provided ready targets. It was especially easy to portray slavery as a negation of Christian morality since the antislavery movement meshed with the rural resentment of urban wealth and agrarian aristocracy.[44]

Popular literature and abolitionist tracts painted the plantation owner as an idle and besotten duelist whose unspeakable lusts and cruelties had free rein over defenseless slaves. By both way of life and livelihood, the slaveholder stood accused as the most dire threat to Christian order. He was, in short, an unmitigated and unredeemed sinner. The cotton economy exercised a tyranny over other Americans and the planter drew his riches from the unrewarded toil of a class of unfortunates. The South became the "Slave Power" and focus of moral outrage.

Of course, antislavery sentiment was by no means universal and the range of feeling in any community was wide and varied. What was true of the community-at-large pertained to the churches as well. Some of Seneca Falls's denominations, such as the Methodists, were relatively united and gave powerful witness to their convictions. The Presbyterians were somewhat less forthright. Slavery was certainly condemned by the Presbyterian congregation, and funds were even allocated to publish the declaration of condemnation in New York State's leading religious journals, the *Observer* and the *Evangelist*. But the resolution never appeared in print outside Seneca Falls and it may

[44]See, e.g., Craven, "The Northern Attack on Slavery," in *Ante-Bellum Reform*, pp. 22–23, 27–28, 35–38.

have been quashed by some members of the Session. In any event, having passed a resolution, many Presbyterians evidently felt they had done their full duty to the abolitionist movement. Others were far less restrained than the Presbyterians. From the late 1830s on, the Methodists passed and forwarded numerous resolutions calling for disfellowship from those of their brethren who tolerated the "peculiar institution." In July 1839, the Seneca Falls Conference reacted boldly to the Georgia, South Carolina, and Baltimore Conferences' effort to deemphasize John Wesley's prohibition of slaveholding:

Reverend Fathers and Brethern the Quarterly Conference of Seneca Falls Station desire to address you on the Subject of Slavery . . . for consideration of the next General Conference.

We love and revere the Methodist ministry. . . . Still, as you have taught us, a death-like Silence, and a cowardly inaction does not become us in any good cause—We must absolutely must encounter the *Devil* whether he roars like a lion or sings like an angel of light.

We believe sumthing [*sic*] effectual may be dun [*sic*] to save the Church from Slavery . . . an evil acknowledged on all hands to be the most complicated and destructive of all evils. . . . When you received us into the Church fellowship, we submited [*sic*] to your examination and one of your test articles was a forbidding to buy and sell men, women and children. . . . We cheerfully subscribed To this aricle [*sic*], But now fearing that the doctrine contained in it and corroberated [*sic*] by other parts of the discipline is going into disrepute in the Methodist Episcopal Church. . . .

We believe that many of our ministers & people are so startled at what they deem wrong and precipitate among abolitionists that fearing for the unity of the Church, they have so directed all there [*sic*] Councils for the Suppression of abolitionism. . . .

In view of the long standing evil of slavery in our church existing in opposition to her genius, Spirit & doctrines as well as the letter of her discipline in opposition to the consciences & better judgment of the Slaveholders themselves—and the feelings of

every uncontaminated, & truly enlightened mind, under the whole
heaven.

We believe the time has arrived when the best counsels of the
Church should concentrate there [sic] wisdom and energies, not
. . . to quell the prevailing Solicitude or subdue & punish abolitionists as to devise some measures which may free the Methodist
Episcopal Church from an evil which "Mr. Wesley calls the sum of
all villanies."[45]

Presbyterians, perhaps for good reason, were loath to go so
far. The mood of disfellowship and the active antislavery sentiments of the Seneca Falls Methodist congregation had bred disunity and, ultimately, division. Unwilling to rupture the national church, the General Conference of the Methodist Church
tried to dampen antislavery attitudes. In response, the Seneca
Falls church claimed "the imperious duty . . . to express their
solemn conviction on moral subjects . . . especially when other
bodies with whom they are connected by ecclesiastical ties, adopt
measures and sanction principles, which . . . are subversive to
the dearest interests, both of humanity and religion . . . as we
believe several acts of the last [1839] General Convention were."
This preamble was followed by five resolutions that, among
other things, demanded acceptance of testimony by "colored"
church members, denounced the Georgia Conference for de-
nying the moral evil of slavery, and insisted that the whole
church proclaim the unquestionable sinfulness of slavery which
"is justly an abiding reproach to any church that tolerates its
existence with its pale." Perhaps more telling was their defense
of the Reverend LeRoy Sunderland, editor of *Zion's Watchman*
and member of Theodore Weld's coterie of religious abolitionists. Sunderland had been tried by the General Conference
many times, and Seneca Falls Methodists were indicting their
national leadership when they defended Sunderland as one
who desired "the purity of the church and evidenced true . . .

[45]All quotations here and below from Quarterly Conference Minutes of the
Methodist Episcopal Church of Seneca Falls, July 27, 1839, November 10,
1840, August 10, 1842, Mand UA, CU.

devotedness to the church and public . . . disinterestedness in the cause of the downtrodden slave . . . and uprighteness and Christian demeanor in his general course."

At last, in 1842, the Seneca Falls Methodists could no longer sustain these tensions. Yet another resolution was sent forward to the Genesee Annual Conference restating "our bounden duty to express our decided conviction that the time has come when more efficient measures should be taken to wipe off the reproach brought upon the M.E. Church by tolerating the evil within our pale." They urged "such measure . . . to separate from our communion those who persist in retaining as property human beings . . . that nonslaveholding conferences may be separated from those who encourage it." When Methodist Episcopal authorities refused to exclude proslavery apologists, the Seneca Falls church was polarized and activists formed the separate Wesleyan Methodist Church in which the Bements found a haven after Rhoda Bement was excluded from the Presbyterian Church.[46]

In the Presbyterian Church of the United States, division over doctrinal differences if not over slavery occurred early and in 1837 culminated in the formal partition of the church into the Old and New School factions. Eventually the two parts of the national Presbyterian church split over the slavery issue, but they did so considerably later than other popular denominations. Some New School Presbyterians created the antislavery Synod of Free Presbyterian Churches in Ohio as early as 1847. Not for another ten years, however, did the New School wing of the Presbyterian church experience the major schism that produced the United Synod of the South. Old School Presbyterians, always more conservative, divided only in the face of

[46]The formation of the Wesleyan Methodist Church took place in March 1843, some five months prior to the Bement affair, and is mentioned in the trial as the factor necessitating a review of the Presbyterian membership to determine whether other defections had occurred. See also, *History of Seneca County*, p. 113 and the unpublished typescript history of the Methodist Episcopal Church of Seneca Falls in the records of the church.

war when, in 1861, the Presbyterian Church in the Confederate States was formed.[47]

The forces of disunity that began to emerge among Presbyterians in the 1830s were largely a reflection of the controversy over the New Measures of Finneyite revivalists. Conservative Presbyterians were most closely attuned to the Scotch-Irish tradition of their church with all its antipathy toward the Yankee heritage of Jonathan Edwards and his successors. They looked to Princeton College for more orthodox Calvinist theological guidance and found their greatest support among the churches of Pennsylvania and the Appalachian region. A large part of the Presbyterian church had little zest for the Arminian influences so characteristic of the church in New England and New York.[48] Geographical distinctions were mirrored by doctrinal combat between the Princetonians and their more radical brethren at Yale and in the seminaries of western New York and Ohio. This quarrel intensified the perennial wrangling in the Presbyterian General Assemblies and in numerous heresy trials. When the General Assembly met in Philadelphia in 1837, sympathizers with the conservative Old School had a majority and excluded some four New School synods, including almost half the national membership of the church. The New School formed a rival assembly after failing to reassert itself in Philadelphia. Both the Old and New School assemblies attracted additional synods, the New School chiefly south of the Ohio River, and each assumed an almost national scope.[49]

Presbyterian schism not only generated doctrinal tensions, but also led to disputes on the issue of social reform. Conserva-

[47]See Marsden, *The Evangelical Mind*, pp. 88ff.
[48]Evangelism reflected the persistent movement from the neo-Calvinism of the late eighteenth century toward the espousal of open Arminianism. The Arminian doctrine that "God saved those who persevered to the end and damned those who continued in disbelief" was a prescription for free will and the active role of the sinner in his own rebirth. See Robert H. Nichols, *Presbyterianism in New York State: A History of the Synod and Its Predecessors* (Philadelphia, 1963).
[49]See Marsden, *The Evangelical Mind*, pp. 59ff.

49

tive adherents of the Old School frequently empathized with those who stood aloof from or actively opposed social and political experimentalism. One suspects that the doctrine of the elect was applied to politics and reform as well as to religion. Some Old School ministers, at least, were hostile to abolition in the North and friendly to the "peculiar institution" in the South. Such was the case of the Reverend William Swan Plumer, with whom Abby Kelley linked the name of Horace Bogue. Conservative clergy were also uncomfortable with the egalitarian tendencies of the frontiers and the industrializing cities. Ministers identifying with the Old School might well find themselves at odds with various elements in their congregations, especially with those who coupled religious conviction with a commitment to social reforms.

Despite the intensification of feeling in regard to abolitionism, the residents of Seneca Falls were not of a single mind on this or other issues. Abby Kelley lectured in the village on at least two occasions and enlisted a number of sympathizers. She was an assertive woman and advocated not only abolition but temperance and, by her very presence, a wider role for women in public life. She was not universally popular. The *Seneca Falls Democrat* damned Kelley with faint praise when she spoke in the summer of 1842: "The somewhat celebrated Abby Kelley addressed the good people of this village last evening [July 27th]. We believe she made a generally favorable impression upon those who heard her—especially upon those who coincide with her sentiment."[50] The *Democrat's* obvious conclusion was that many did not "coincide with her sentiment."

Antebellum reformers certainly saw Negro bondage as the "great evil," yet they recognized that slavery came in many guises. Alcohol could often be a crueler master than the slaveowner and its power over men was daily visible to the people of Seneca Falls. The churches stood in the front lines of the war on drink, and church members who compromised with

[50]*Seneca Falls Democrat*, July 28, 1842.

alcohol by using it in moderation or winking at its sale were open to special opprobrium. There were even some who, like the Bements and the Matthewses, looked askance at communion wine. Most church members were delighted when secular organizations took up the temperance crusade.

Temperance in the 1830s and 1840s sought to rehabilitate the prosperous as well as the poor. Recognizing that drunkenness was not a problem unique to impoverished laborers, the middle class sought to reform itself and drew upon the lessons of religious experience. The temperance meetings resembled religious revivals, but took on a more secular character as laymen allied themselves with evangelical Protestants in the war on the "demon rum." In the 1840s a group of "reformed men," ex-alcoholics who hoped to bring others to the joy of abstinence, organized themselves as the Washingtonians. Other groups such as the Good Templars and the Sons of Temperance eventually supplanted the Washingtonians but kept the same commitment to middle-class values. Claiming nearly a quarter-million dues-paying members, the Sons of Temperance pledged themselves to total abstinence.[51]

Between February and July 1842, the Washingtonian movement in Seneca Falls spawned a temperance newspaper appropriately named the *Water Bucket*. Flavius J. Mills and a reformed drunkard, John Jay Davis, were its publishers. Amelia Bloomer, writing as "Gloriana," was its most famous contributor.[52] An early issue linked temperance and abolition as two fronts in the common war against the shackling of the human soul. "Alcohol enslaves the body and mind . . . enslaves individuals, families and communities . . . it is a far more inexorable master than the southern planter—for he generally supports his slave in their [*sic*] old age—making more sufferable their exit from a life of servitude and wrong."[53] Servitude was the

[51]Joseph R. Gusfield, "Temperance, Status Control and Morality," in *Ante-Bellum Reform*, pp. 128–130.
[52]*Occasional Papers of the Seneca Falls Historical Society*, 1905.
[53]*Water Bucket*, April 22, 1842.

common charge against society; to free men from the fetters of sin was the first step toward the elimination of this condition. Abolitionism, the temperance movement, and the demand for women's rights were only varied facets of the same struggle to liberate American society.

America's promise was thwarted as a few selfish interests wrung their profits from the community as a whole. Not only the individual rum drinker and his family suffer, it was declaimed, but the entire community assumes the cost of their affliction. The editors of the *Water Bucket* were certain that "there would be no lower classes, if it were not for rum drinking."[54] Moreover, they used Seneca Falls itself as primary evidence. Before the formation of the Washingtonians, one justice of the peace recorded seventeen assaults, twenty-four petty offenses, and thirty-one cases requiring outdoor relief during one seven-month period. The same justice credited the temperance movement with reducing assaults by almost two-thirds and nearly eliminating petty offenses and calls for relief.[55] Though selfish rum sellers and the indifference of some influential men made temperance more difficult, the *Water Bucket* felt there was cause for optimism. "Fortunately for the temperance soldier, he is not under the necessity of looking to some distant period for the accomplishment of some single victory . . . for every step of his march is cheered by some success."[56]

The *Water Bucket* was a short-lived publication originally designed to prepare the village for a major temperance rally. The celebration, held on the Fourth of July 1842, was a characteristic strategy aimed at arousing the community's conscience. Organizers included several prominent members of the Presbyterian Church along with representatives of other denominations.[57] Both newspaper and rally reflected the objectives of the Washingtonians and advocated teetotalism. Members of the

[54]Ibid., June 10, 1842.
[55]Ibid., May 6, 1842.
[56]Ibid., February 25, 1842.
[57]Ibid., June 14, 1842.

movement were former drunkards who pledged "entire abstinence," and the *Water Bucket* echoed their sentiments: "Even
cider will induce a love of something stronger, and so the natural tendency is to desire an increase of strength, it will increase
the danger of relapse."[58] To be sure, not everyone in Seneca
Falls shared so complete a commitment.

The *Democrat,* whose editor participated in the July 4th rally,
sounded a far more cautious note. Announcing formation of
an Independent Temperance Society, Josiah Miller "trusted"
that the new society's "zeal will in all cases be tempered with
moderation, and that they will never forsake the powers of
persuasion for those of coercion, legal or otherwise."[59] Washingtonians were less concerned with niceties. The *Water Bucket* ap-
plauded the appointment of Edward S. Latham, a "cold-water"
man, as superintendent of the Seneca and Cayuga Canal. They
were confident he would compel "entire abstinence" and "allow
no lock tender or person in his employ to keep a rum shop
along the Canal from which death and destruction may be
dealt out for three cents a drink."[60] Many supported temperance; fewer wanted to push the cause beyond persuassion,
witness, and exhortation. As in other reforms, there was a di-
chotomy between those whose zeal demanded action and those
accepting individual conversion and example.

John Timmerman was one who sought to extend temperance. Along with Rhoda Bement and her brother, Elias Denison, as well as Dr. Charles Williams, he conducted the "scien-
tific" experiment whose results were used as evidence to accuse
the minister and elders of the church of introducing distilled
spirits into the very house of God! One suspects that the out-
come of the experiment was spread throughout the congregation as a means of bringing the church members to a stricter
view of temperance. Timmerman was a village laborer and president of the Independent Temperance Society, which drew

[58]Ibid., June 10, 1842.
[59]*Seneca Falls Democrat,* September 23, 1841.
[60]*Water Bucket,* February 25, 1842.

members chiefly from the "mechanic" class but also boasted the support of more distinguished men—the lawyer-publisher Dexter Bloomer for one.[61] The *Water Bucket*, moreover, criticized those "*very respectable*!! opponents of temperance" and rejoiced that they had "taken the alarum. . . . They feared their power is gone, they fear that the scales are falling from men's eyes, and that those whom they heretofore looked upon as but instruments of their own unholy designs are about to exercise the attributes of freemen."[62] In reading the transcript of Mrs. Bement's trial, one senses that she and her associates viewed Rev. Horace Bogue and many of the elders as "very respectable" but not altogether dedicated to the cause of temperance.

To settle for mere persuasion was hard when, in the reformer's mind, liquor threatened the very fabric of community. As in most antebellum American communities, the purveyance of alcohol was common enough. The village "boasted" some three thousand citizens and their taste for strong drink was satisfied by two distilleries, a large brewery, and thirty or more "rum shops." Despite easy access to alcohol, Seneca Falls registered more temperance pledges than any other town in the state. Thirteen hundred men and women pledged "entire abstinence" and it was a "temperance village" indeed.[63]

In 1839 the village Board of Trustees had licensed liquor retailers, chiefly grocery stores, and limited their sales to five or more gallons per customer. In July 1841 the Seneca Falls Temperance Society was founded. It grew to seventy-five members in one month and less than a year later carried nearly five hundred names on its roster. Neither of Seneca Falls's political parties was willing to risk antagonizing such a large number of temperance folk, and in the election of 1842 all nominees of both parties opposed the further granting of liquor licenses. Whereas twelve licenses had been issued in 1841, the village

[61]*Seneca Falls Democrat*, July 29, 1841, and August 12, 1841; *Water Bucket*, February 25, 1842.
[62]*Water Bucket*, August 5, 1842.
[63]Ibid., February 25, 1842.

granted none in 1842, the only town in the county that refused to do so.[64] Two years earlier, the board had gone on record as opposing "the retail and use of intoxicating drinks . . . an evil more productive of more misery, crime & poverty than all other causes . . . a greater tax upon the inhabitants of this village than all other taxes . . . we now appeal [to liquor retailers] . . . to discontinue a practice so opposed to the interests of the taxpayers of the village . . . and we do hereby pledge ourselves to sustain the *Best* of the village in using all lawful means to suppress the same."[65]

Antilicensing campaigns reflected the conviction that public temperance could not be achieved by moral suasion and personal witnesses alone. The Timmermans, Lathams, Bements, Denisons, and their allies advocated more forceful policies. Earlier calls for abstinence fell short of swearing off fermented beverages: beer, wine, or cider. Since alcohol was important to local retailing—grocers, druggists, and even hardware stores kept a jug or two for the convenience of their customers— banning its sale would seriously effect village merchants. Nonetheless these temperance advocates condemned *all* liquors whether distilled or fermented and pressed for legal restraint of the "rum traffic" in each state. The first state to respond, Massachusetts, in 1838 prohibited liquor sales in lots of less than fifteen gallons. Mill hands and laborers were unlikely to buy their booze wholesale. Reformers strove to bring this compulsory morality to New York State as well.[66]

Through both its moral imperatives and its call to social action, revivalism provided weapons to attack the wickedness of strong drink. Less an expression of lingering Puritanism than of a businesslike outlook, temperance joined a moral absolutism with the virtues of industry. It shared with revivalism the values of the rural middle class. Just as the Seneca Falls Board of

[64]Ibid., April 8, 1842, and April 15, 1842.
[65]Minutes of the Board of Trustees of the Village of Seneca Falls, May 5, 1840, Village Clerk's Office, Seneca Falls.
[66]See Gusfield, "Temperance, Social Control and Morality," in *Ante-Bellum Reform*, p. 134.

Trustees labeled liquor retailing as conducive to "misery, crime & poverty" and "opposed to the interests of the taxpayers," so the upward-striving middle class castigated the drunkard for his idleness and waste of community resources. Drink dissipated energies and distracted men from the proper aspiration to do well and prosper. Since the drinker's family demanded charity, the community also suffered. Moreover, in an economy based on credit and mutual trust, rum made men poor risks. Intemperance was a character fault and religious conversion aimed at a total change of habits. The drive to abstain entirely, even from suspect communion wine, mirrored the absolute nature of conversion and underlined nineteenth-century America's faith in the power of the human will. "Entire abstinence" and immediate abolition were both part of the ethos of revival.

Yet, as with abolition, there was a tension between reformers and those who feared the disruptive effect of the immediate arrival of the New Jerusalem. Few, argued openly with the aims of the temperance movement but many questioned its methods. The refusal to license the sale of liquor and the attempt to institutionalize temperance by laws were seen by some as an attempt to substitute coercion for voluntary compliance. For those who were committed to the principles of free enterprise and the liberty of the individual, this approach smacked of the heedless sacrifice of traditional freedoms in the interest of moral absolutism. To some, the militancy of the temperance movement seemed to dragoon one segment of the community—a segment of considerable economic importance—in order to strike the shackles from another—one which was perhaps reluctant to escape its bonds. In freeing the community of the burden of strong drink, temperance workers sought a social transformation of dizzying proportions. It was not a change everyone was willing to accept without qualification.

To the extent that the supporters of abolition and temperance sought liberation from the past, they also countered the desire for stability. This juxtaposition of conflicting aims fostered discord within the churches and within the larger com-

munity. Impatience with the inertia of cautious leaders im-
pelled many reformers to adopt increasingly strident positions:
they demanded not only an end to slavery but immediate abolition, not merely temperant behavior but "entire abstinence."
The position taken on these issues became, for them, a test
of moral and religious commitment—a test that few people
could pass and that many people resented. Consequently, the
militant spirit of evangelical "immediatists" was often thwarted
by the cautiousness of those Christians who feared that uncontrolled enthusiasm threatened to disrupt communities and might
very well delay the achievement of social perfection.

4

The struggle for emancipation, whether from arrogant southern planters or the cynical merchants of the liquor trade, inevitably produced resistance if pushed too far or too fast. In
the village of Seneca Falls, Rhoda Bement's challenge to the authority and integrity of Rev. Horace Bogue served to focus these
issues in a single moment and to highlight yet another struggle—the struggle for the rights of women. Rhoda Bement's
world was dominated by a militant paternalism that denigrated
the humanity of women, stifling their capacities and their ideal-
ism. Thus, when women such as Abby Kelley, the Grimké sisters, and Rhoda Bement asserted their right to be heard and to
act in public, they did violence to one of the most powerful
traditions of their time.

Conventional wisdom labeled women as less rational than
men and more prone to emotional extremes. Such reasoning
essentially relegated women to a decorative place in public life.
When the Presbyterian Session characterized Rhoda Bement as
"unlady-like," their prejudices were obvious. Her outspoken
and conscientious defiance had violated their mores, and they
now asked her to accept passively woman's "place" in the social
structure. Whether from the pew or the rostrum, activist women

were less than welcome to many men. First, feminine assertion implied a runaway enthusiasm disruptive of good order. Second, it challenged male authority and the dignity of pastoral leadership in the churches. In short, females were likely to breed controversy as well as babies. And once it became public, controversy imperiled the reputation of a church and its governance. Even reformers saw an outspoken woman as a dangerous force that might well undermine public support for their cause.

As in many a small and changing community, Seneca Falls's religious leaders needed to tread cautiously in dealing with such women. To carry moral commitment beyond the stage of individual conversion was threatening enough to many ministers. But for a woman, and an extremist at that, to champion social reform was to gallop far in advance of village mores. In the view of a careful man, pastor or layman, an Abby Kelley threatened to divide the congregation and polarize opinion. Such is the concern that seems to be reflected in the question put to Jabez Matthews during the Bement trial: "Whether he as a Presbyterian considered it proper for a *female* to call a *promiscuous* meeting for the purpose of addressing them on Moral & Religious subjects."[67] Seneca Falls shared the common bias against nineteenth-century female assertiveness. The local newspaper felt no embarrassment in offering the complacent advice that a "good" wife ought to display three characteristics:

[67]Except for the Quakers and isolated instances of irregular female preachers among aberrant Baptist and Methodist congregations, organized religion permitted women virtually no authoritative voice in church affairs. The terminology used in the question clearly appealed to this sort of prejudice, and perhaps connoted contempt for women. The word "promiscuous" seems to have several connotations. First, it refers to the irregularity of women expressing themselves on "moral and religious" subjects. Second, it suggests that a woman who steps outside the sphere of domestic life is somehow notorious and disreputable. For example, the *Seneca County Courier,* reporting on September 22, 1840, that a woman had made a political demonstration, concluded that "a female who could thus degrade herself and her sex, for any purpose whatever, is really to be pitied; and the man who would incite her to such an act, merits the scorn and contempt of all." For similar attitudes in Utica, New York, see Ryan, *Cradle of the Middle Class,* pp. 78ff.

First . . . be like a snail, always keep within her own house. . . . Second . . . be like an echo, to speak when she is spoken to; but like an echo she should not always have the last word. . . . Third . . . be like a town clock, always keep time and regulation; but she should not, like a town clock, speak so loud that all the town may hear her.[68]

Abigail Kelley, an associate of the Grimké sisters who was active in the abolition and temperance movements during the 1840s and 1850s. Courtesy the American Antiquarian Society, Worcester, Massachusetts.

However modestly women testified in public to their support of abolition or other reforms, it was a discordant note in a male dominated community.

Horace Bogue was affiliated with the American Colonization Society, which female abolitionists such as the Grimkes decried

[68]*Seneca Falls Democrat*, April 2, 1840.

S. H. GRIDLEY, D. D.

The Reverend Samuel H. Gridley and his residence in Waterloo, New York. Gridley was appointed temporary moderator of the Seneca Falls Presbyterian Session to conduct the trial of Rhoda Bement. From *History of Seneca Co., New York* (Philadelphia, 1876), reprinted by W. E. Morrison and Co. (Ovid, New York, 1979).

as not "loving" blacks. To oppose the institution of slavery was one thing, to imply a common and equal humanity with blacks was quite another. Many endorsed the antislavery movement as

Dr. Joseph Kerr Brown, an elder of the First Presbyterian Church of Seneca Falls who was appointed Rhoda Bement's defense counsel after the resignation of her original choice. Courtesy Seneca Falls Historical Society.

an assault on aristocratic privilege and a wicked way of life; far fewer wanted to elevate blacks to citizenship and respectability. The attitudes of the Grimkés and their allies were anathema to the leaders of an essentially conservative community. In the

61

case of Abigail Kelley, a militant abolitionism merged with a powerful note of anticlericalism. Her contempt for the "establishment" clergy's lethargy and indifference toward reform was

Mrs. Ansel Bascom, a minor witness at the Bement trial who testified to the "Moral & Religious" nature of Abby Kelley's lecture. Courtesy Seneca Falls Historical Society.

extended to organized religion and shared by at least some radical abolitionists.

Prejudice against women served as a bridge between the abolition movement and women's rights. Revivalism had taught the value of action and association in the achievement of goals. It had, in some measure, provided a wider scope for the expression of women's intellectual capacities and served as a model

The First Presbyterian Church of Seneca Falls, site of the Bement trial, as it appeared about 1850. Original drawing based upon early engravings in the Seneca Falls Historical Society.

for the organization of female antislavery groups. Yet a large portion of the abolition movement tried to keep women in the background. It labeled public service "unwomanly" and accused women who sought it of violating the "woman's sphere."[69] The

[69]Lerner, *The Grimké Sisters*, pp. 161–162, 166.

The First Baptist Church of Seneca Falls as it appeared in the mid-nineteenth century. The church was the site of several revivals in the late 1830s, and Rhoda Bement was a member until she joined the Presbyterian Church in 1839. Courtesy Seneca Falls Historical Society.

female struggle for emancipation from the burden of traditional laws, property rights, education, employment, and morality traces its formal beginnings to 1848, when Lucretia Mott and Elizabeth Cady Stanton issued a call for the Seneca Falls

The Methodist Episcopal Church of Seneca Falls as it looked at about the time of the Bement trial. Courtesy Seneca Falls Historical Society.

Women's Rights Convention. The consciousness that emancipation was necessary, of course, long predated the convention. It found expression in the readiness of individual women to affirm their dignity by both personal witness and deed.

The Wesleyan Methodist Church of Seneca Falls, an interior view showing several of the congregation, ca. 1850. The group may include some of those who defected from the Methodist Episcopal Church about seven years earlier. Courtesy Seneca Falls Historical Society.

The Grimké sisters, Sarah and Angelina, were drawn into the women's rights crusade through their antislavery activities. Angelina was a prominent and convincing abolitionist lecturer as were Sarah and others such as Abby Kelley. Angelina had been the first woman to address any American legislature. Her speech before the Massachusetts State Assembly in 1838 attracted overflow crowds and was preceded by a scurrilous campaign of ridicule and caricature. The impact of her speech, however, established a tie in the public's mind between aboli-

East view of Seneca Falls village.

The village of Seneca Falls, ca. 1840. The "Flats," seen in the center of this early engraving, were subsequently covered by a lake formed by damming the Seneca River. Courtesy Seneca Falls Historical Society.

tion and women's rights.[70] Unfortunately, the subsequent schism in the antislavery movement made it more and more difficult for the Grimkés and other women to express their commitment on public platforms.

When the Anti-Slavery Convention met in Boston in 1838, it was seriously divided on the question of female leadership. Urged on by William Lloyd Garrison, the convention decided to accept women as members and then went so far as to elect

[70]Ibid., pp. 1–6.

The "Old Stone Shop," erected by Jeremy Bement and his partner in 1829 as a carriage factory. In the wake of the 1837 Depression, the structure was purchased as a pump factory and eventually became the site of Seabury S. Gould's first industrial enterprise. Courtesy Seneca Falls Historical Society.

The Sackett Block, a group of retail stores erected by the prominent developer Gary V. Sackett. In the background, beyond the bridge, is one of Seneca Falls's several distilleries. Courtesy Seneca Falls Historical Society.

Abby Kelley to one of its committees. Garrison's opponents fastened on the "woman question" to attack his policies and his domination of the movement. Accused by his detractors of distracting supporters by forcing the consideration of "irrelevancies," Garrison was also denounced for foisting on the mem-

MOHAWK AND CAYUGA
Packet Boats.

THE subscribers, in order more fully to accommodate the public, have determined upon starting a boat from Schenectady for Cayuga and the Seneca Falls, regularly every SATURDAY, during the season. This is intended merely as an addition to their establishment, and will in no wise interefere with their usual business—as boats and waggons will as heretofore be kept in constant readiness to transport from the city of Albany to any part of the western country, either by land or water, whatever property may be directed to their care. Gentlemen who reside at a distance from the water communication, are informed that their goods will be delivered from the boats at any place they may think proper to designate ; and at the Seneca Falls, to avoid delays, waggons are provided to convey the property, if required, to its place of destination. Every effort will continue to be made, to afford their customers the most perfect satisfaction, and from their long experience in this line of business, they hope to merit the public patronage.

Eri Lusher & Co.

A typical advertisement for travel between the East and Seneca Falls. Packet boats were usually given priority on the canal and generally carried passengers and "fast freight." Courtesy Seneca Falls Historical Society.

This view looking west along the canal in Seneca Falls shows the manufacturing activities that lined its banks. The lock in the center was used to raise and lower barges over the falls of the Seneca River. Courtesy Seneca Falls Historical Society.

The village of Seneca Falls in the winter. The river and canal are frozen, putting a temporary end to navigation. The river flowed to the south and the canal to the north of the "Flats," which have long since disappeared under Van Cleef Lake. Courtesy Seneca Falls Historical Society.

bership what they considered an "outspoken and domineering feminist." The anti-Garrison forces left the Massachusetts Anti-Slavery Society and formed a rival bloc under the Reverend Amos Phelps. One year later, they constituted a separate orga-

A raceway along the Seneca River. The round opening in the building in the center of the picture allowed the escape of water after it flowed over the mill-wheel. Courtesy Seneca Falls Historical Society.

nization, the Massachusetts Abolition Society. That same year, the conflict was extended to the national meeting and the entire movement was fractured. As the antislavery movement developed during the 1840s, women were increasingly excluded

73

A Seneca Falls flouring mill as it appeared about midcentury. The millrace is seen in the center of the picture with several canal barges shown on the far left. Courtesy Seneca Falls Historical Society.

Cowing and Co., one of Seneca Falls's leading industrial enterprises, seen from across the Seneca-Cayuga Canal. Cowing engaged in the manufacture of pumps and fire engines and represented the new industrial character of the village. Courtesy Seneca Falls Historical Society.

from leading roles. Their active participation was held suspect as "unwomanly" and sometimes disparaged as ineffectual. Many women now began to appreciate the fact that blacks were not the only creatures in need of emancipation. There is a direct line from the battle against slavery to the demand for women's rights.

Temperance, too, was a vitally important issue for women reformers. Alcohol was a customary, even necessary, part of daily life for a majority of Americans, but its widespread use had especially harmful consequences for women. Since women were legally and traditionally dependent upon husbands and fathers, drunkenness threatened them both personally and through its impact on the well-being of their families. Many women were therefore eager to participate in the crusade against strong drink, yet too often they were denied a leading role. In Seneca Falls, for example, such leading feminists as Amelia Bloomer contributed their talents and intelligence to the temperance movement, but its leadership remained firmly male. Despite the tremendous impact of alcohol abuse on women, the problem was posed in masculine terms and little was done to understand the issue from a feminine perspective or to deal specifically with the needs and problems of women. Rhoda Bement was unique when she shared the lead in pressing the issue of temperance in her church. By questioning the nature of the communion wine and, by implication, accusing her minister and the elders of moral laxity, she went beyond the bounds of accepted female behavior.

Though Rhoda Bement's violation of accepted norms was an affront to ministerial dignity, she was acting in accordance with the evangelical spirit of American Protestantism. Revivalism had generally encouraged the participation of women with men in "mixed" prayer meetings and often allowed women a leading place. It is not surprising, given the numbers of women active in all churches, that they sought a mode of expression more dynamic and challenging than audible response at Sunday meet-

76

ing.[71] The mushrooming of women's organizations for both revival and benevolence testifies to their organizational and managerial potential.[72]

Since the dynamics of religious enthusiasm denied feminine passivity, revivalism served as a training ground of women activists. Substantially more women than men experienced conversion.[73] Perhaps revivals offered an opportunity for escape from dependence: if women "belonged" to their husbands, at least their souls could be liberated. Some were content to leave the formation of church policy to men; yet, when women like Rhoda Bement found policy in conflict with conscience, it was hard to remain silent. For doctrinaire clerics or even ordinary male traditionalists, the assertiveness of women coupled with the extension of enthusiasm beyond the limits of individual religious conversion must have seemed revolutionary indeed.

The central theme of the Rhoda Bement trial is the stress generated by the desires for both change and stability. Her challenge to the authority of the male leadership of her church confronted Seneca Falls's Presbyterians with the threat of disunity at a time when harmony was perceived as vital to preserving the influence of the church in the community. The church men and women of Seneca Falls recognized the danger of disintegration in a village already subject to considerable stress and thought of themselves as a nexus of good order. Faced with a threat to harmony, the authorities of the church drew back from activism. Choosing caution, the Reverend Horace Bogue reluctantly brought his parishioner to trial.

[71]See, e.g., Ryan, *Cradle of the Middle Class*, pp. 75ff, and Cross, *The Burned-Over District*, p. 38. See also, Ann Douglas, *The Feminization of American Culture* (New York, 1977).

[72]For an excellent model of the study of the relationship between religion and social activism, see Kathryn Kish Sklar, *Catherine Beecher: A Study in American Domesticity* (New Haven, Conn., 1973).

[73]The records of the First Baptist Church of Seneca Falls for the series of revivals taking place during the late 1830s give ample testimony to the numbers of women converted; see also, Ryan, *Cradle of the Middle Class*, appendix C.2, p. 257.

PART TWO

The Trial of Rhoda Bement

TRANSCRIPT FROM THE SESSION OF
THE FIRST PRESBYTERIAN CHURCH
OF SENECA FALLS

Dramatis Personae

WILLIAM ARNETT, a thirty-five-year-old (all ages are given as of the year of the trial), moderately successful miller. Arnett had joined the Presbyterian Church in 1835 and was to become a ruling elder in 1850. He was elected President of the Board of Trustees of the Village of Seneca Falls in 1843.

MRS. ANSEL BASCOM, wife of the prominent Seneca Falls attorney Ansel Bascom. Mrs. Bascom was a pillar of Trinity Episcopal Church. She and her husband actively promoted women's rights, abolition, and other social reforms.

MATTHIAS BELLOWS, a fifty-five-year-old physician. Bellows joined the Presbyterian Church in 1843 and became a ruling elder in the same year. The head of a large, prosperous, and active family, Bellows was president of the village Board of Trustees in 1840 and 1844. He proved cantankerous and contentious in both church and community affairs, and was excluded from the Presbyterian Church in 1851.

JEREMY BEMENT, a thirty-six-year-old carriage maker. Bement had joined the Presbyterian Church in 1839. His questionable business practices (he failed in the 1837 Panic) caused problems for him both in and outside the church. Nonetheless, he did serve on the village Board of Trustees in 1837 and 1846. Bement left Seneca Falls for Buffalo in 1849 and died of cholera in that year.

RHODA BEMENT, born Rhoda Denison of Stephenton, New York, she married Jeremy Bement in 1830. Mrs. Bement had joined the Baptist Church in 1838 and left to join the Presbyterian a year later. She left Seneca Falls with her husband in 1849.

REV. HORACE P. BOGUE, born in Winchester, Connecticut, he was forty-seven in 1843. Bogue was ordained in 1823 and served as minister in Gilbertsville, New York (1823–29), Norwich, New York (1829–33), and Vernon, New York (1833–40). Before coming to Seneca Falls in 1842, he served for two years as an agent of the New York Colonization Society. The society's "acceptance" of the institution of slavery may have prompted Miss Kelley's criticism. Bogue left Seneca Falls in 1850 and later served as a Jewish Missionary and as an agent in Liberia. He died in 1872.

DR. JOSEPH KERR BROWN, a fifty-year-old physician and druggist. Brown joined the Presbyterian Church in 1835 and was chosen a ruling elder four years later. A trustee of the village in 1842 and 1843, he became president of the board in 1847. In 1849 Brown left Seneca Falls for Lockport, New York.

MOSES C. DEMING, a forty-year-old druggist and physician. Deming joined the Presbyterian Church in 1843 and was chosen a ruling elder in that year. Deming was a village trustee in 1839. He died in 1845.

ELIAS DENISON, a farmer in his thirties. Denison had joined the Baptist Church in 1839, was constable of the village in 1839 and 1840 and also served as street commissioner. In 1841 Denison appears in the newspaper as an abolitionist elector of Seneca County. He died in 1847.

MISS L. DENISON, Elias Denison's daughter and Rhoda Bement's niece. She was a teenager and evidently had no denominational affiliation.

PRUDENCE DOUGLASS, a teenage servant girl who worked and boarded with the Bements. Douglass had come to Seneca Falls from Ludlowville, New York, and joined the Presbyterian Church in 1841. In 1844, after apologizing to the church for refusing the communion cup and failing to attend church services, Douglass received a letter of dismission from the session.

ABBY DUMONT, a thirty-seven-year-old boardinghouse keeper. Dumont had joined the Presbyterian Church in 1827.

SERING W. EDWARDS, a forty-nine-year-old farmer. Edwards had joined the Presbyterian Church in 1831. During a long and distinguished career in community service, Edwards was town supervisor, superintendent of the poor, militia officer, and commissioner of highways. He died in 1876.

DANIEL W. FORMAN, a lawyer and businessman in his forties. Forman had joined the Presbyterian Church in 1830 and became a ruling elder in 1832. He also served as superintendent of the Sabbath School. Forman was the secretary of the Seneca County Anti-Slavery Society in 1839 and appears as an abolitionist elector in 1840.

WILLIAM FOX, a sixty-year-old farmer. Fox was a longtime member of the Presbyterian Church; he appears to have had some difficulty with the church in 1823.

HARRIET FREELAND, the thirty-eight-year-old wife of a carriage maker (William Pitcher). She had joined the Presbyterian Church in 1831.

SALLY FREELAND, the thirty-two-year-old wife of Elbert Lindsley. The couple worked a farm near Seneca Falls. Freeland had joined the Presbyterian Church in 1831. She died in 1885.

REV. WILLIAM GRAY, minister of the Presbyterian Church from 1835 to 1838. Gray was close to sixty at the time of the trial.

REV. SAMUEL H. GRIDLEY, a forty-one-year-old Presbyterian minister. Girdley served congregations in Perry, New York (1830–36), and Waterloo, New York (1836–73).

CORNELIUS HOOD, a thirty-three-year-old owner of a coalyard that supplied the railroad. He had joined the Presbyterian Church in 1841 and was chosen a ruling elder the next year. In 1846 Hood accused Bogue of heresy, was suspended and excommunicated, but was allowed back into the church in 1852 and was chosen a ruling elder the next year. Hood was an abolitionist.

ABIGAIL (ABBY) KELLEY, twenty-eight-years-old at the time of the trial. She had converted to abolitionism while a teacher at a Friends school in Providence, Rhode Island, and was active locally until 1837. At the first women's antislavery convention in New York in 1837 she met the Grimké sisters. She made her first public address before a "mixed" audience in 1838, and subsequently became a well known abolitionist lecturer. Her lecture at Seneca Falls in 1843 came when she was at the peak of her career. In 1841 she had resigned from the Society of Friends because of their lukewarm position on slavery. Her lectures were characterized by a strong anticlerical note. In the 1840s she met and married Stephen S. Foster, a New England radical of strong anticlerical inclinations, and they frequently traveled as a team. Not limiting herself to the antislavery movement, Kelley also espoused the causes of temperance and feminism. In generally poor health after the 1850s, she was capable of only limited activity in the last quarter century of her life. She died on January 22, 1887.

WILLIAM KING, a fifty-one-year-old investor and speculator of considerable wealth. King had joined the Presbyterian Church in 1828. Although under frequent suspicion for unethical business practices, he was chosen a ruling elder in 1842. King served as village firewarden and trustee.

ELEANOR LUM, in her forties at the time of the trial. The wife of hat manufacturer and retailer David B. Lum, she had joined the Presbyterian Church in 1831. Convinced of the imminent end of the world, Mrs. Lum became a Millerite and was excommunicated from the church in 1846.

DELIA MATTHEWS, in her forties and the wife of Jabez Matthews, she had joined the Presbyterian Church in 1826, left for the Congregational Church in 1834, returned to the Presbyterian Church, and left again for the newly formed Congregational Church in 1852.

JABEZ MATTHEWS, a fifty-year-old manufacturer and tradesman. Matthews had joined the Presbyterian Church in 1830, left for the Congregational Church in 1834, returned to the Presbyterian Church, and left again for a newly formed Congregational Church in 1852. Matthews appears in the newspapers in 1840 as an abolitionist elector of Seneca County.

HUGH MCALISTER, a seventy-eight-year-old former tavernkeeper. McAlister had joined the Presbyterian Church in 1817 and become a ruling elder in 1818. McAlister was engaged in frequent controversies over business in church and elsewhere. In 1837 Jeremy Bement charged him with falsehood and fraud in the purchase of a wagon. McAlister was found guilty but the Session was reluctant to punish a man who "for so long a time" maintained "a regular standing." McAlister died in 1850.

HUGH MCALISTER, JR., a farmer in his thirties who had joined the Presbyterian Church in 1831. He appears to have resided in West Fayette, New York, from 1838 until 1841, when he returned to Seneca Falls. McAlister left the community in 1846.

JONATHAN METCALF, a farmer and entrepreneur in his fifties. Metcalf had been one of the founders of the Baptist Church in 1828 and the first president of its Board of Elders. By the late 1830s, presumably because of the issue of slavery, Metcalf joined the Methodist Church, where he remained until 1844, when he presumably joined the Wesleyan Methodist Church. In 1840 Metcalf was president of the Seneca Falls Abolitionist Society.

THOMAS J. PAINE, a forty-year-old canal boat supplier and candle and soap manufacturer. Paine was associated with the Methodist Church until his withdrawal in 1840. After that his denominational affiliation, if any, is unknown. He was village trustee in 1845 and 1846.

CORNELIA PERRY, arrived from Chittenango, New York, in 1841 with her storekeeper husband, Henry. They joined the Presbyterian Church in 1843.

ALEXANDER S. PLATT, a seventy-seven-year-old farmer. Platt had joined the Presbyterian Church in 1839 and was immediately elected a ruling elder. He died in 1844.

JOHN POOLE, a forty-nine-year-old Scotsman who worked in a

factory. Poole joined the Presbyterian Church in 1843 and was chosen village sexton in 1844. In 1852 he was charged with neglect of ordinance, intemperance, "profaneness," licentiousness, and violation of the sabbath. When he twice failed to appear to answer the charges, the Session excluded him.

ISAAC RACE, a sixty-six-year-old carpenter. Race had joined the Presbyterian Church in 1839, appears to have lived in Connecticut from 1839 until 1841, and returned to Seneca Falls in 1841.

FANNY SACKETT, thirty-five-year-old daughter of William Sackett, patriarch of the most prominent family in Seneca Falls. She had joined the Presbyterian Church in 1831.

BETSY SQUIRES, probably the daughter of farmer Nicholas Squires. She had joined the Presbyterian Church in 1831.

JAMES SQUIRES, probably the son of Nicholas Squires. He had joined the Presbyterian Church in 1831 and was chosen a ruling elder in 1844.

MRS. MARK SQUIRES, probably Mary Squires, who had joined the Presbyterian Church in 1831.

JOHN TIMMERMAN, a laborer in a boatyard who does not appear to have had a denominational affiliation. Timmerman was president of the Independent Temperance Society in 1841.

REV. H. VAIL, the regular minister of the Seneca Falls Presbyterian Church from 1839 until 1843.

THOMAS VAN ALSTYNE, a forty-eight-year-old businessman. Van Alstyne had joined the Presbyterian Church in 1831. He subsequently left for Prattsburg, New York, but returned in 1836 and rejoined the Presbyterian Church. Van Alstyne died in 1847.

DR. CHARLES D. WILLIAMS, a forty-year-old physician. Williams came to Seneca Falls from New York City in 1835. In 1841 he was expelled from the Medical Society for practicing homeopathic medicine. Williams' expulsion caused a furor in Seneca Falls. Williams left Seneca Falls in 1842, but remained in the area and became secretary of the Homeopathic Medical Society of Western New York in 1843.

A Note on the Text of the Trial

What follows is the text of the trial of Rhoda Bement. The words of testimony are important in the understanding of village attitudes and mores and warrant close attention; equally significant is the more subtle evidence of the trial's texture. The emphases, the priority of the charges and evidence, the style of language and the nuance—all are vitally important to an interpretation of the events surrounding Rhoda Bement's confrontation with her church. So far as possible, we have reproduced the original manuscript. Although the recorder's spelling and punctuation were often inconsistent, they remain unchanged. Where the secretary's omissions or idiosyncracies seemed to confuse the meaning of the text, we have added clarifying words or phrases. Accurate reproduction of a questionable or incorrect word in the original is indicated by using the device *sic*. All editorial additions are bracketed; all parentheses are found in the original manuscript. Certain terms used in the trial had very precise meaning to the participants and we offer the following definitions drawn from the *Constitution of the Presbyterian Church in the United States of America* (1842 ed.), pps. 409–410, 415-417, 450:

1. A Presbyterian church *session* consists of all pastor(s) and ruling elders of a particular congregation. "The Church session is charged with maintaining the spiritual government of the congregation; for which purpose, they have power to inquire into the knowledge and Christian conduct of the members of the church; to call before them offenders and witnesses, being members of their own congregation, and to introduce other witnesses where it may be necessary to bring the process to issue, and when they can be procured to attend; to receive

members into the church; to admonish, to rebuke, to suspend, or exclude from the sacraments those who are found to deserve censure; to concert the best measures for promoting the spiritual interests of the congregation; and to appoint delegates to higher judicatories of the church."

2. The *moderator* was usually the pastor of the congregation and possessed "all authority necessary for the preservation of order; for convening and adjourning the judicatory; and directing its operations according to the rules of the church." When for "prudential reasons" it is not appropriate that the pastor be the moderator, the pastor (with the concurrence of the session) may invite another minister, belonging to the same presbytery, to preside.

3. The *ruling elder(s)* were "properly the representatives of the people, chosen by them, for the purpose of exercising government and discipline, in conjunction with pastors or ministers."

The Trial of Rhoda Bement

Session Met Oct. 2, 1843[1]
Present Rev. H. P. Bogue Mod.
H. McAlister, A. S. Platt   Opened with Prayer
D. W. Forman, C. Hood
M. C. Deming & J. K. Brown Eld.

Minutes of the last meeting read and approved.

The committee to whom was refered the resolution on the subject of American Slavery[2] presented the following report (see document on file—Amer. Slavery) which was accepted and unanimously adopted. On Motion Resolved that we have a recess until after the meeting of the Church which is to be held this afternoon at 2 o'clock.

Meeting of the Church. Opened with prayer by the Pastor.

Minutes of the last meeting from which this was adjourned read and approved.

[1]The authority under which the session met and subsequently charged Rhoda Bement was based upon *The Constitution of the Presbyterian Church in the United States of America Containing the Confession of Faith, the Catechisms, and the Directory for the Worship of God: together with the Plan of Government and Discipline, as Ratified by the General Assembly, at their Sessions in May 1821; and amended in 1833* (Philadelphia: Presbyterian Board of Publication. Paul T. Jones, Publishing Agent, 1842).
[2]We cannot locate the text of this resolution, although it is clear from the church records that it condemned slavery.

The resolution on the subject of American slavery coming up in order. Thereupon on the call of one of the members the Session presented a preamble & resolution expressive of their views of the subject, which was unanimously adopted by the church as their action thereon. On Motion Resolved that there be three hundred copies of the resolution on the subject of American Slavery published in pamphlet form for distribution among the members of the Church. And also that it be published in the *New York Observer* and *New York Evangelist*[3] & that the expence of the whole be paid from the funds of the Church. After prayer the meeting of the church was adjourned.

Meeting of Session resumed.

It having come to the knowledge of Session, that a transaction had occured involving the christian reputation of Mrs Rhoda Bement, by the presentation of a paper of which the following is a copy (to wit):

1st Common fame[4] charges Mrs. Rhoda Bement with having been guilty of a very unchristian outrage towards the acting Pastor of this Church on the 1st Sabbath of October 1843 in the vestibule of the church & in the presence of many members of the congregation.

2[ndly] Common fame charges Mrs. Bement with *falsehood* uttered on that day.

1st In affirming that Mr. Bogue knew that a certain notice of hers was in the desk on that day before he had dismissed the congregation, when in truth Mr. Bogue knew no such thing.

2nd In affirming that Mr. Bogue had rec[d.] a notice of hers upon the last Sabbath of Sept. & refused to read it & then upon the Monday following had called a meeting of the Session for the especial purpose of laying the subject mat-

[3]Church resolutions were frequently published in these two newspapers. The antislavery resolution of the First Presbyterian Church of Seneca Falls apparently did not appear.

[4]The term "common fame" refers to charges, rumors, or occurrences widely circulated within the congregation or community. Charges may be brought either by an individual member of the church or by "common fame."

ter of said notice before them; or to get them to take order in regard to it, when every part of the statement is untrue.

3rd In affirming that Dr. Brown and Mr. Bogue in visiting her husband a short time previous went with one thing on their lips, while they had another thing in their hearts. She asserted that they were not honest—All of which is untrue.

3^{rdly} Common fame charges Mrs. Bement with having been guilty of slandering the Pastor of this Church & members of the Session.

1st In stating publicly that she had reason to believe that the Pastor of this Church had been dishonest in regard to not presenting her notices, or in saying that he had not received them.

2nd In saying that Dr. Brown and Mr. Bogue in visiting her husband had not been honest men; that they went with one thing on their lips & another thing in their hearts.

3rd In asserting that the Session of the Church had been convened under such circumstances & for such an object as if generally believed would expose them to scandal & contempt. Therefore on Motion Resolved that a committee be raised to visit Mrs. Bement & report to session at their next meeting. Resolved that D. W. Forman, M. C. Deming & J. K. Brown constitute such committee. Adjourned.

Closed with Prayer

J. K. Brown Clerk

Session Met Oct. 13, 1843

· · · ·

The Committee appointed to visit Mrs. Bement made the following report (to wit): On visiting Mrs. Bement she states that she addressed Mr. Bogue in the porch in order to ascertain why two notices she had sent up were not read. The conversation was as follows as far as Mrs. Bement recollects: I asked Mr.

Bogue why he refused to read the notice I laid on the desk? He said he saw no notice. I asked him how it could be he did not see the notice when it lay before him on the desk? Said he, I see a paper but did not read it till after I dismissed the congregation. I asked him if some one did not tell him that I laid it on the desk & if that wasn't the reason he did not open it? He said no. I asked if it wasn't his practice to open papers to see if it was anything which ought to be read? In answer to that he says: Mrs. Bement, I think your course a very improper one from the beginning. I think you very unchristian, very impolite and very much out of your place to pounce upon me in this manner. I told him I thought differently. I thought I had a right to put the notices on the desk & to ask him why he didn't read them.

Then he repeated again that it was very unladylike & very unchristian to pounce upon him in that manner and he said: you seem to doubt my veracity, the truthfulness of what I say. This he repeated more than twice, as I believe (that is, that I doubted his veracity) before I answered. I then said: Mr. Bogue I'll tell you why I doubt it. You told me you was an abolitionist & I supposed if you was an abolitionist you would read abolition notices that were bro't here. I bro't one last Sabbath and it wasn't read. He said he saw no notice. I said then a special meeting of session was called on Monday morning at 10 A.M., I supposed, to look into the matter. For the next day following, Mr. Bogue and Dr. Brown visited Mr. Bement & the charge they bro't against him was for not attending the third service, when I believed it was for attending an abolition meeting. [And] Dr. Brown admitted in the conversation there was not a male member of the congregation attended all the meetings as regularly as Mr. Bement. [And] the Church very well knew there was not a family in the place which attended as regularly as we did. Yet the charge was for not attending the third service & I do not think it was honest. Then Mr. Bogue called upon them all to witness the conversation, he was not a going to let it pass by so.

In commencing the conversation it was between Mr. Bogue and myself, without any intention to have it public & no one could have heard except Mr. Hugh McAlister Jr., as the conversation was in a low-tone, untill Mr. Bogue in his replies spoke in such a tone as excited the attention of the bystanders. I had no idea of saying anything more, than to ask him the question why he refused to read the notices, & should not if I had not been led on by Mr. Bogue's remarks. The whole conversation was without any excitement on my part, or any indications of feeling or excitement, unless it might have been looked upon as such an indication that I called upon Mr. Bogue to hear me through. [And] upon doing so I raised my hand as Mr. Bogue started to go off. When I had this conversation with Mr. Bogue, I did suppose the Session had the meeting alluded to, with a view to a course of discipline in the case of Mr. Bement & others. [And] I was never undeceived in that respect untill the committee called upon me, when Dr. Brown informed me it was not so.

I did also at that time suppose that the charge made against Mr. Bement by Dr. Brown & Mr. Bogue when they called, was for not attending the third service & was confirmed in this from what my husband had said, who labored under the same impression. In respect to this also Mr. Bogue did not undeceive me.

Resolved that the report of the committee be accepted. On Motion.

Resolved that a committee be raised to inquire further into the matter &, if thought necessary, to table charges & present the names of witnesses. On Motion.

Resolved that M. C. Deming & Mr. Bogue be such committee.

Adjourned.   Closed with Prayer
                                              J. K. Brown Clerk

Session Met Dec. 1, 1843   On Notice
Present Rev. H. P. Bogue Mod.
D. W. Forman, M. B. Bellows   Opened with Prayer
M. C. Deming, C. Hood & J. K. Brown Elders

Minutes of the last meeting read and approved.

. . . .

Committee in case of Mrs. Rhoda Bement made the following report (to wit):

General Charge

Common fame charges Mrs. Rhoda Bement with disorderly & unchristian conduct.

1st In employing improper language towards the acting Pastor of this Church upon the 1st Sabbath of Oct. in the vestibule of the Meeting House & in the presence of a number of the members of the congregation.

2nd In publicly affirming that Mr. Bogue knew that a certain notice of hers was in the desk on the first Sabbath of Oct. before he dismissed the congregation—which is untrue.

3rd In persisting publicly to affirm that Mr. Bogue must have known the notice was in the desk after having been solemnly assured by him that he knew no such thing.

4th In publicly affirming that Mr. Bogue had rec[d] a notice of hers upon the last Sabbath of Sept. & had refused to read it—Which is utterly false.

5th In publicly declaring that the Pastor of the church had called a meeting of the Session on the Monday following the last Sabbath of Sept. for the particular purpose of getting them to take action in regard to her notices—all of which is entirely untrue.

6th In persisting publicly to affirm that the Pastor had rec[d] her notices & had convened the Session to take order in regard to one of them, after having been distinctly informed by the Pastor himself that she was entirely mistaken in regard to the whole matter.

94

7th In publicly asserting that she had reason to believe that in what the Pastor had said & done in regard to the above mentioned notices & the above named meeting of the Session he was not an honest man—All of which is utterly untrue.

8th In asserting publicly that Dr. Brown & Mr. Bogue in visiting her husband a short time previous to the 1st Sabbath in Oct. were not honest men. That they had visited him with one thing on their lips & another thing in their hearts— All of which is untrue. On Motion.

Resolved that the report of the committee be accepted. On the question of adoption, On Motion:

Resolved that it lie over untill the next meeting of Session. On Motion:

Resolved that we adjourn untill the 8th inst. at 10 o'clock A.M.

Adjourned.   Closed with Prayer
                              J. K. Brown Clerk

Session met Dec. 8, 1843   On Adjournment
Present Rev. H. P. Bogue Mod.
M. B. Bellows, A. S. Platt,   Opened with Prayer
D. W. Forman, M. C. Deming,
C. Hood & J. K. Brown Eld.

Minutes of the last meeting read & approved.

. . . .

The case of Mrs. Rhoda Bement coming up in order & after consultation & discussion. On Motion:

Resolved that we adjourn untill the 18th inst. at 10 o'clock .A.M.

Adjourned.   Closed with Prayer
                              J. K. Brown Clerk

Session met Dec. 18, 1843   On Adjournment
Present Rev. H. P. Bogue Mod.
A. S. Platt, M. B. Bellows   Opened with Prayer
D. W. Forman, C. Hood
M. C. Deming & J. K. Brown Eld.

Minutes of the last meeting read & approved.

. . . .

The case of Mrs. Rhoda Bement coming up in order. On Motion:

Resolved that the motion now before us (being on the question of adoption) lie on the table for the purpose of reconsidering the vote of acceptance.

Resolved that the vote accepting the report of the committee be reconsidered.

The following communication was presented by Alexander S. Platt, a member of the Session (to wit):

I charge Mrs. Rhoda Bement with disorderly & unchristian conduct.

First in dividing the Lord's Supper, partaking the bread & refusing the cup.[5]

Second in attending in a conspicious manner upon the exhibitions made by Abby Kelley on the first Sabbath of Aug. last between the hours of five and eight o'clock P.M. & while the church to which Mrs. Bement belongs were attending upon divine service.

Third in her behavior towards the Pastor of this church in the vestibule of the church on the first sabbath of October last in the presence of various members of the congregation.

Fourth in absenting herself from the communion on said first sabbath of October.

Fifth in having absented herself from public worship since that time whenever the acting Pastor of said church has officiated.

I further state that though I supposed it unnecessary to take

[5]The Lord's Supper, or communion, is a sacrament which, in Protestant churches, commemorates Christ's Last Supper and subsequent redemptive sacrifice. The sacramental act involves the symbolic consumption of the body and blood of Christ, through the eating of bread and drinking of wine.

the first step of labour[6] alone with Mrs. Bement, still I proposed to her to do so, but she waived the right. I have, therefore, in company with Brother Race taken the necessary steps to bring this matter before the Session & have obtained no satisfaction.

Seneca Falls Dec. 11, 1843   Signed A. S. Platt

The committee to whom was refered the case of Mrs. Bement report that in consequence of the charges exhibited by Mr. Platt against Mrs. Bement, no further report from them is deemed necessary. On Motion:

Resolved that the report of the committee be accepted. On Motion:

Resolved that the Clerk cite Mrs. Rhoda Bement to appear before Session at their next meeting to answer to the charges prefered against her by A. S. Platt. On Motion:

Resolved that when we adjourn we adjourn to the 27th inst. at 10 o'clock A.M.

Whereas it having come to the knowledge of this session that Sally Freeland & Harriet Freeland now Mrs. Lindsley and Mrs. Pitcher have united with the Wesleyan Methodist Church[7] in this village. Therefore:

Resolved that their names be stricken from the list of members of this church. On Motion:

Resolved that there be a committee of three raised to examine the records of this church & ascertain who of its members are in the habit of neglecting its ordinances & institutions & to report anything that may be proper for the session to take cognisance of. On Motion:

Resolved that D. W. Forman, C. Hood & J. K. Brown constitute such committee.

Adjourned.   Closed with Prayer

                                              J. K. Brown Clerk

[6]Before charges can properly be filed, the complainant must, through discussion and exhortation, attempt to settle the dispute amicably and privately. The accused may waive his or her rights to be "labored with," and insist upon a trial.

[7]Founded in March 1843 as an offshoot of the Methodist Episcopal Church, the Wesleyan Methodist Church was more militantly antislavery than any other church in Seneca Falls.

Session Met Dec. 27, 1843   On Adjournment
Present Rev. H. P. Bogue Mod.
A. S. Platt, D. W. Forman,   Opened with Prayer
M. B. Bellows, M. C. Deming
J. K. Brown Elders

Minutes of the last meeting read & approved.

Mrs. Rhoda Bement appeared before Session on citation.

Resolved that the Session now proceed to take up the case of Mrs. Bement.

Whereupon the usual charge in such cases to the Judicatory was announced by the Moderator. On Motion:

Resolved that Mrs. Bement be furnished with a copy of the charges & the names of the Witnesses.

The question being put to the parties by the Moderator whether they were ready to proceed to trial, Mr. Platt replied that he was not, the witnesses not having been cited.

Whereas Mrs. Bement made the request that her husband be allowed her counsel. Therefore on motion:

Resolved that her request be granted & that Mr. Bement be such counsel.

Consent of the accuser being obtained. On Motion:

Resolved that Mrs. Bement be allowed to plead to the charges, which she did in the following communication which she read to the session (to wit):

I am not conscious of being guilty of disorderly and unchristian conduct.

Neither has my accuser ever pointed out to me the *disorderly & unchristian* conduct of which he complains. Nor has he or any other brother ever conversed with me on some of the subjects mentioned in his charge & specifications.

And he never even intimated that he was aggrieved or had come to labour with, or had ought against me. And moreover, neither do any of the specifications following the charge sustain it nor do they describe any disorderly or unchristian conduct.

First—I cannot conscientiously take of the cup unless it contains the fruit of the vine, as used and authorised by our Lord himself.

Second—Exhibitions made by Abby Kelly! It is right? Is it honest? So to misname a christian discourse, a gospel lecture on the duty of christians, & the condition of God's poor. Who could ever *dream* or imagine from the record what was meant by this charge. [And] yet, it was mainly showing christians their duty to carry the glad tidings of liberty & salvation to 2 1/2 millions of human beings held in worse than Egyptian bondage, & that we of the north are the slaveholders.

Third—Does not mention a single word or fact of the conduct or conversation, & therefore cannot be replied to, proved or disproved, & ought to be dismissed.

Fourth—Has my accuser ever inquired whether I was sick or had some other good & sufficient reason for being absent on said day[?]

Fifth—This like all the other specifications is an attempt to bind the conscience & deprive me of christian liberty contrary to the confession of Faith page 90 & Church Government 345.[8]

And now I ask does it not look more like an attempt to *crush* than to reclaim an erring member (if I have been guilty of error).

And I appeal to brethren to say whether it be right, whether it is kind & whether it is christian? Thus to attempt to destroy a person's christian character contrary to the *rules* laid down in the word of God, & the constitution of the Presbyterian Church.

Resolved that this case stand adjourned untill the 12th day of

[8]"God alone is Lord of the conscience, and have left it free from the doctrines and commandments of men which are in anything contrary to his word, or beside it, in matters of faith or worship. So that to believe such doctrines, or to obey such commandments out of conscience, is to betray true liberty of conscience; and the requiring of an implicit faith, and an absolute and blind obedience, is to destroy liberty of conscience, and reason also."

"that the Holy Scriptures are the only rule of faith and manners; that no church judicatory ought to pretend to make laws, to bind the conscience in virtue of their own authority; and that all their decisions should be founded upon the revealed will of God" (*The Constitution of the Presbyterian Church*, pp. 90, 345).

Jan. next at 10 o'clock A.M. & that the Clerk issue the proper citations to the parties & witnesses.

Resolved that the session concur with the Pastor in inviting the Rev. Mr. Gridley to Moderate this session in the onward progress of this trial.

Adjourned.   Closed with Prayer
                                                      J. K. Brown Clerk

Session met Jan. 12, 1844   On Adjournment
Present Rev. S. H. Gridley Mod.
H. McAlister, A. S. Platt,
M. B. Bellows, M. C. Deming   Opened with Prayer
& J. K. Brown Elders

Minutes of the last meeting read & approved.

The case of Mrs. Rhoda Bement coming up in order, & on inquiry being made by the Moderator, if the witnesses had been cited & if the parties were ready to proceed to trial. [And] these questions having been answered in the affirmative, The Moderator again charged the Judicatory respecting the case now before them.

Whereas an objection was raised to Mr. Bement being the counsel of Mrs. Bement in the further progress of this trial & being decided by the Moderator that he could not be such counsel. Whereupon Mrs. Bement stated to the session that she could not proceed at this time, & gave notice that she wished Elder D. W. Forman who was now absent to be her counsel. Therefore on Motion:

Resolved that we adjourn untill the 23rd inst. at 10 o'clock A.M.
Adjourned.   Closed with Prayer
                                                      J. K. Brown Clerk

Session Met Jan. 23rd 1844   On Adjournment
Present Rev. S. H. Gridley Mod.
H. McAlister, A. S. Platt
D. W. Forman, M. B. Bellows   Opened with Prayer
C. Hood, M. C. Deming &
J. K. Brown Elders

Minutes of the last meeting read & approved with the exception of the word "further" in the 7th line from top of Page 144.

The case of Mrs. Bement coming up in order and the question being put by the Moderator if the parties were now ready. Each declared on their part they were.

Resolved that D. W. Forman a member of the Judicatory at the request of Mrs. R. Bement be assigned her counsel in the course of this trial.

The first specification. Moderator put the question to Mrs. Bement through her counsel: admits the fact & the reason given was that she acted from conscience in this case not knowing that it was the fruit of the vine.[9]

[Hood]   Cornelius Hood being duly sworn says: I have witnessed in passing the elements of the Lord's Supper to Mrs. Bement that she has refused the cup once & perhaps twice.

[Gridley]   Question by Moderator: Did you pass the cup to Mrs. Bement yourself?

[Hood]   Ans.: It was passed by her Husband. Confident that she did not accept.

[Bement]   Question by Accused: Did you ever converse with Mrs. Bement on this subject?

[Hood]   Ans.: I have & the reason given by her was she has scruples of conscience and that she did not think it contained the fruit of the vine & if it was it contained alcohol or some kind of drug.

[Gridley]   Have you yourself or do you know of any other one who has ever visited with Mrs. Bement to converse with

[9]"Fruit of the vine" refers to wines naturally fermented, without the addition of distilled spirits.

her on this particular subject before the commencement of this prosecution:

[Hood] Ans.: I do not.

[Judicatory] Question by the Judicatory: Did Mrs. Bement say she knew it was corrupt wine?

[Hood] Answer: The impression I obtained from her was she did not consider it the pure juice of the grape & could not use it on Temperance principles.

[Judicatory] Do you know that Mrs. Bement refused the cup from what you saw & from her admissions to you?

[Hood] Ans.: I do.

[Bement] By Accused: What do you know of your own knowledge?

[Hood] Ans.: I know she did not partake of the cup.

[Bement] What were her admissions to you?

[Hood] Ans.: She said she had conscientious scruples & that she did not think it was the fruit of the vine & if it was, it contained alcohol or some kind of drug.

Read to witness & approved.

[Forman] D. W. Forman sworn, says: I passed the emblems on one occasion at which time I cannot say she refused the cup at that time or not. Within a very few days from that time in conversation with her she stated that it was the last time she could partake of the cup. The reason she assigned for taking that step was that it was not the fruit of the vine & she could not conscientiously partake of it. And in the same conversation she stated that she did not believe it was consistent with her views respecting Temperance. She has recently stated that she has not partaken for nearly two years and that she took that course conscientiously, believing that the fruit of the vine only was to be used as the emblem & that the material used did not contain any portion of the fruit of the vine, that it is a manufactured article consisting of alcohol & other drugs.

[Judicatory] Did Mrs. Bement inform you at the time how she came to the knowledge it was poluted and not genuine?

[Forman] Ans.: She was informed by reading that such wine was manufactured & that there was little if any other came into the country. She had read from a paper a receipt for making it, showing there was not a particle of wine in it. This she said was her view of the wine used on sacramental occasions & that she was confirmed in this opinion by an experiment on wine procured at Doctor Brown's Store. Which experiment resulted in a tea saucer full or half pint of alcohol to one pint of wine.

[Judicatory] Whether you as a member of the Session knowing the difficulty under which Mrs. Bement laboured did you ever converse with her on the subject?

[Forman] Ans.: In the conversation above alluded to in which she said she could not use such wine, I told her she should not wound her conscience in what she did, but had subsequently tried to show her her duty.

[Bement] Question by Mrs. Bement: Did I or did I not say to you that I supposed the wine on which the experiment was tried to be the same used at the communion?

[Forman] Ans.: I understood Mrs. Bement to say she supposed it was that wine or such wine as was used at the communion.

[Judicatory] Elias Denison, being duly sworn: Do you know respecting the wine distilled by Timmerman?

[Denison] Ans.: Was in the room when the experiment was made but did not examine the wine nor go up to examine the process of distillation.

[Judicatory] What was the result of the wine from which the experiment was made?

[Denison] Ans.: Something more than one saucerfull paper dipped in it would burn—burning off the alcohol & leave the paper clean.

[Judicatory] Do you know anything of the wine used at the different churches for communion?

103

[Denison]   The only wine that I have seen in Seneca Falls that had, as I believed, any of the juice of the grape in it.

[Judicatory]   What proportion of Brandy or alcohol do you suppose it contained? What was the character of the wine?

[Denison]   Ans.: When undiluted I thought it a very strong & rich wine. Suppose it may contain 50% of alcohol undiluted, though my opinion may be erroneous.

[Judicatory]   Will the smell of it be sufficient to produce intoxication?

[Denison]   There have been times in my life when it would sensibly affect me and there have been times when the affect would be only pleasant & agreeable & would not produce intoxication.

[Judicatory]   By the Judicatory: Did you ever take any of that wine in your mouth?

[Denison]   Ans.: I have.

[Judicatory]   Did it have the effect upon you that it would to take spirits of wine into the mouth?

[Denison]   Ans.: It does not have the same effect as pure alcohol.

[Judicatory]   Do you know positively that the article experimented upon by Dr. Williams or by Mr. Timmerman was the same article procured from Dr. Brown?

[Denison]   I do not know as it was, as I did not procure it.

[Judicatory]   In making up your mind on this wine, what makes you suppose it contained 50 per cent of alcohol?

[Denison]   Ans.: From the taste of the article, what I have read, and from being once in my life quite a wine drinker & also from experiments made in this place.

[Judicatory]   Do you suppose from the taste of that wine that it contained more alcohol than the high wines of our common distilleries?

[Denison]   Ans.: Not more.

[Judicatory]   Do you think that it contains more alcohol than whisky at proof?

[Denison]   Not more. In speaking of the proportion of alcohol contained in the wine should have said proff [*sic*] spirits.

[Brown]   J. K. Brown, being duly sworn, says: That he has furnished the wine used at the communion of the church for nearly four years. That he procured through the agency of another in the city of New York, an article of Madeira wine such as he supposed an imported article. That the application was made to have an article procured expressly for communion, & that it must be as pure an article as could well be obtained. The agent employed was a man who had been brot [*sic*] up to the business & considered himself a proper judge of wine. That he did some time since sell a pint of Madeira wine on the prescription of Doctor Williams[10] & was afterwards informed the same was experimented upon by Mr. Timmerman. But this wine so sold on such prescription was not any of the wine first alluded to. It was an article taken in exchange & when so sold told the person particularly I did not consider it pure wine.

[Judicatory]   Question by Judicatory: Have you provided the wine for the last three or four years for the communion of this church?

[Brown]   Ans.: I have.

[Bement]   Question by accused: Do you know the character of the wine used at the communion?

[Brown]   Does not, but my best impressions are that it is the juice of the grape.

[Bement]   What was the cost of that article?

[Brown]   Thinks it was two dollars and fifty cents.

[Bement]   What is the price of the best kind of wine?

[Brown]   Ans.: Have seen lately in the papers of Madeira wine sold by the dealers at from three to five dollars pr. gallon.

[10]J. K. Brown, the town druggist, sold alcoholic beverages but admonished his customers in newspaper ads that stated: "Alcoholic beverages for sale, for medicinal uses, and that only."

[Bement] Was not the price of wine higher four years ago than now?

[Brown] Should think not. Have understood that imported wine or Liquor is much higher now than then.

[Bement] Is wine ever sent into the country in a pure state?

[Brown] Ans.: I suppose rarely.

[Bement] Have you diluted the wine with water when used at the communion?

[Brown] Ans.: I have.

[Bement] How large a proportion at any time?

[Brown] Ans.: One half. Witness knew it was fermented wine consequently contained alcohol & at the suggestion of members of different churches in this village did prepare it as above stated. This course was suggested as the wine was rich and would be made better by dilution.

[Judicatory] By the Judicatory: Do you suppose that to be as pure wine as could reasonably be procured in the country at this time?

[Brown] Ans.: I intended it should be so.

Read & Approved.

In this stage of the case Mr. Forman from ill health was excused from acting any further as Mrs. Bement's counsel & on motion J. K. Brown was assigned as her counsel in the future progress of this trial.

Resolved that in consequence of the transfer of J. K. Brown as counsel for Mrs. Bement that M. C. Deming be clerk pro tem.

[Brown] *Defense* Mrs. Matthews was duly sworn. By Defense: What was the effect of the wine on you the last time you partook of it?

[Matthews] The last time I partook of the wine it was very offensive; it was very strong alcoholic wine. I have been absent the last two communions and at the two previous

communions I refused to partake of it. Reasons, consciousness [*sic*]. Read to the witness & approved.

Mrs. Lum was duly sworn: Question the same as asked Mrs.
Matthews.

[Lum]   Ans.: I always smell it as soon as poured out. It produces a flush & either sick or nervous headache. I have
often remarked to my Husband that I did not wonder
reformed men[11] were or should be afraid to taste or remain
in the House when the wine was poured out. That it produced the same effect on me as alcohol does when used
mechanically. It always produces headache.

[Gridley]   Question by Moderator: Is this the sick Headache?

[Lum]   Some-times, not always.

[Gridley]   Are you subject to the Headache?

[Lum]   Ans.: Yes, either sick or nervous.

Read & approved by witness.

[Brown]   Miss P. Douglass was duly sworn by Defense. Question: Are you a member of the Bement's family?[12]

[Douglass]   Yes.

[Brown]   When you are present at the communion season what
is your relative situation as to Mr. & Mrs. Bement?

[Douglass]   Ans.: I sit between them.

[Brown]   Does Mr. Bement pass the cup to Mrs. Bement?

[Douglass]   I have not see him pass it for some time.

[Brown]   Have you ever heard Mrs. Bement complain of Headache as complained by Mrs. Lum?

[Douglass]   Ans.: Have not.

[Brown]   What has been the effect in your own case?

[Douglass]   The effect has been unpleasant & the smell dis-
agreeable.

[11]Temperance organizations, particularly the Washingtonian movement, sought
to enlist confirmed drunkards, and required a signed pledge of total abstinence
from these "reformed men."

[12]In the pre-Civil War era the term "family" referred not only to blood rela-
tives, but also included boarders and co-resident employees.

[Gridley]   Question by Moderator: How long since you partook of the cup?

[Douglass]   Ans.: Nearly a year. Reason, I could not take it conscienciously. Have felt symptoms of Headache. Conscious [*sic*] scruples, the main reason.

[Session]   Question by Session: Are you acquainted with different kinds of wine?

[Douglass]   I am not. Smells like alcohol to me.

[Gridley]   Question by Mod.: Have you ever complained to any of the officers of this church?

[Douglass]   I believe I mentioned it to Mr. Forman.

[Gridley]   Did you endeavor to ascertain whether they got the best kind of wine?

[Douglass]   Did not.

[Gridley]   Did you ever entertain the idea that you were breaking convenant with the church in refusing the cup?

[Douglass]   Ans.: I have not. I felt I could not conscientiously partake of it.

Read to witness & approved.

[Judicatory]   Jonathan Metcalf sworn: What kind of wine are you in a habit of using in the Methodist Church?

[Metcalf]   Ans.: For the last year they pressed grapes & used the unfermented juice. Boiled it & diluted it properly.

[Judicatory]   Do you suppose there is any difficulty in procuring such an article for use?

[Metcalf]   Ans.: We found no difficulty in obtaining any quantity of grapes.

Read to witness & approved.

Second Specification

[Judicatory]   Mrs. Lum: Was you present at the meeting of Miss Kelly?

[Lum]   I was.

[Judicatory]   Did Mrs. Bement take any part, for instance in speaking in the meeting?

[Lum]   Ans.: She did not.

[Judicatory]   Did you hear Mrs. Bement say any thing respecting a meeting at this house at that time?

[Lum]   I never did.

[Session]   Question by Session: Did you stay to the meeting until it broke up?

[Lum]   I did.

[Session]   Did Mrs. Bement sit on the stage?

[Lum]   She did or very near it. She had a seat of some kind.

[Session]   Was that a meeting of discussion of any form?

[Lum]   I do not recollect.

[Session]   Were there any other speakers besides Miss Kelly?

[Lum]   No other one.

[Session]   Was there any Resolution offered?

[Lum]   I think not.

[Session]   Was there any pledge offered for signatures?

[Lum]   Think not at that meeting.

[Session]   Did you hear the Presbyterian Church denounced there as corrupt?

[Lum]   This nation was guilty of slavery & the Presbyterian Church was also guilty as being connected with them.

[Session]   Was this particular church denounced?

[Lum]   Ans.: I do not remember that anything was said in respect to this particular church.

[Session]   Did you hear the Pastor of this church denounced there by name by the speaker?

[Lum]   In speaking of some things that had taken place, she, Miss Kelly, said I happen to know something of your Mr. Bogue the Pastor of the Presbyterian Church. And she asked if he was not connected with the South.

[Session]   Question: Was there a Resolution offered at which some bolted & ran away?

[Lum]   It was not a Resolution as I remember, but in speaking of the churches in general. Mr. Fox took exception & said it was not so. For he had withdrawn from our church and united with another.

109

[Session]   Ques.: Whether Miss Kelly had a pledge?

[Lum]   I have seen a printed pledge before I saw Miss Kelly.

[Session]   Who was considered Moderator?

[Lum]   Did not have any.

[Bement]   Ques. by Defendant: What was the general character of that meeting?

[Lum]   Ans.: I think it was not irreligious.

[Bement]   How was it opened?

[Lum]   By reading a chapter in the Bible.

[Bement]   Was there singing?

[Lum]   Hymn sung, conducted by Christian people.

[Bement]   Did you say there was silent prayer?

[Lum]   Ans.: Miss Kelly said let us have a season of silence.

Read to witness & approved.

On the 2nd Specification Mrs. Bement by her Counsel raised the following objections (to wit):

First—That the book of discipline Ch. 4 Sec. 8 (page 396)[13] requires that the time, place & circumstances should be stated so that the accused may have an opportunity to extenuate or alleviate the offence.

Second—That the records of the session were offered in proof of a resolution passed by session Sept. 25, 1843 to visit certain members of the church & also offered the testimony of that committee to show that they never had visited Mrs. Bement.

Both of which were overruled by the Moderator.

[Judicatory]   Miss F. Sackett sworn: Do you know of Mrs. Bement attending Miss Kelly's meeting on the 1st Sabbath of August between 5 and 8 P.M.?

[Sackett]   I saw her there.

[Judicatory]   Did you hear Mrs. Bement speak there?

[13]"In exhibiting charges, the times, places, and circumstances should, if possible, be ascertained and stated, that the accused may have an opportunity to prove an alibi, or to extenuate or alleviate his offense" (*The Constitution of the Presbyterian Church*, p. 396).

[Sackett]   Ans.: Did not.

[Judicatory]   Have you heard Mrs. Bement say she knew there was a meeting here at the same time?

[Sackett]   Did not.

[Session]   By Session: What was the subject treated on by Miss Kelly?

[Sackett]   Ans.: On national sin.

[Session]   Did she say all the christian churches were involved in that sin?

[Sackett]   Ans.: Yes.

[Session]   Did she denounce the gospel Ministry?

[Sackett]   Not at that time but have heard her at other times.

[Session]   Did she recommend the fear & love of God?

[Sackett]   She did some times & others spoke against the sins of the church.

[Session]   Has the counsel of the accused been to you to have your [*sic*] correct your testimony?

[Sackett]   Ans.: No sir.

[Session]   Has your memory been refreshed?

[Sackett]   Yes. I was told what I said & I wish to correct it.

[Session]   Did you hear the Pastor of this Church denounced?

[Sackett]   I did not. I left before that time.

[Gridley]   By Mod.: Was you pleased with that lecture?

[Sackett]   Ans.: Some parts of it I was.

[Gridley]   What was your views with regard to the profit of that class of Lectures on that day?

[Sackett]   I think that Lectures on Abolition or Temperance are not profitable on the Sabbath.

[Gridley]   Was the doctrine of Abolition or the manner in which she presented it or the things she connected with it the occasion of your dissatisfaction?

[Sackett]   Ans.: With the manner of exhibition & the things connected with it.

[Bement]   By Defendant: Did Miss Kelly in denouncing the church, speak disrespectfully of the church in any manner excepting in speaking of the sins of the church as connected with slaveholding?

[Sackett]   She did not.

Read to witness & approved.

Adjourned untill to morrow at 2 o'clock P.M.
Closed with prayer.

Second Specification   Session Met on Adjournment
Present as before. D. W. Forman appeared
& took his seat as one of the Judicatory.   Opened by Prayer.

[Brown]   For defense: Jno. Metcalf sworn. Do you believe in
   the Christian observance of the Sabbath Day?
[Metcalf]   Yes I do.
[Brown]   Was you present at a lecture of Miss Kellys on 1st
   Sabbath of August last?
[Metcalf]   Ans.: I was present.
[Brown]   Tell us as to the character of the Lecture.
[Metcalf]   It was a moral & Religious Lecture on the subject of
   Slavery and Anti Slavery.
[Brown]   Was any portion of the Bible read then?
[Metcalf]   There was a Chapter portion read I think in Isaia
   [*sic*].
[Brown]   Did Miss Kelly request that any one should lead in
   prayer?
[Metcalf]   Yes.
[Brown]   Was any made?
[Metcalf]   Not vocally.
[Brown]   Then did she request that there should be a season
   of silent prayer?
[Metcalf]   I did not hear it. There might have been such request & I not have heard it.
[Brown]   Was there any singing?
[Metcalf]   There was according to my recollection.

[Brown]   Can you tell us what was sung?
[Metcalf]   I cannot tell the words. It was an Antislavery Hymn.
[Brown]   Have you ever seen that Hymn?
[Metcalf]   I have not.
[Brown]   Who lead the singing?
[Metcalf]   I don't Recollect.
[Brown]   Did a member of the Presbyterian Church lead singing on that occasion?
[Metcalf]   I think it was.
[Brown]   What member?
[Metcalf]   I think Mr. Matthews.
[Brown]   Was the Lecture Religious & Moral?
[Metcalf]   I do [think so]. What I heard. I left before it closed. It exhibited slavery in a moral point of view.
[Brown]   Was the subject for the consideration of religious persons?
[Metcalf]   Yes.
[Gridley]   Moderator: Did you regard the Lecture as profitable?
[Metcalf]   Yes.
[Gridley]   Was it denunciatory?
[Metcalf]   She bore pretty hard & severe on the northern churches.
[Gridley]   Was the language calculated to convince people?
[Metcalf]   It might [have] been clothed in little milder language.
[Gridley]   Was the manner of remark calculated to remove or strengthen prejudices?
[Metcalf]   On some minds it might have strengthened prejudices, on others might have moved conviction.
[Gridley]   Do you think her Lectures on the whole were calculated to do good?
[Brown]   Objected to. Question withdrawn.
[Session]   By session: Was the notice for a Religious Meeting to worship God, or for some other particular purpose?
[Metcalf]   My understanding it was to be an Antislavery Metting or Lecture.

[Session]   Was the accused seated on the stage or platform?

[Metcalf]   I believe she was.

[Session]   In what light did Miss Kelly consider the churches and this among the rest as to the Christian world?

[Metcalf]   She assumed the fact that the American churches were guilty of slavery.

[Session]   Was that such a meeting for the service of God as is contemplated by the Book?

[Metcalf]   I think it was.

[Session]   Were there a number of professed Christians present & do you know of any reason why it was not opened by prayer?

[Metcalf]   No special reason. No clergyman present & not usual for lay members to pray unless called on by name.

[Session]   Is it not usual to commence all religious meetings with prayer?

[Metcalf]   It is with most professing Christians. As to Presbyterians & Methodists it is.

[Session]   What do you consider a religious meeting?

[Metcalf]   When we are taught our duty to God & to our fellow creatures.

[Session]   Is not a religious meeting for the purpose of worshiping God in public?

[Metcalf]   Yes.

[Session]   Was that meeting for the purpose of worshiping God in solemn manner?

[Metcalf]   Yes.

[Session]   Do you believe that God was worshiped there in spirit & in truth?

[Metcalf]   I tried to do so myself.

[Bement]   By Defendant: What did Miss Kelly say that was hard & severe against churches?

[Metcalf]   She said they were guilty of slaveholding. [They] were not Christians if they practiced these things, viz. sold men, women & children.

[Session]   By Session: Did she say that the churches at the north having the majority & having it in their power to put it right were more guilty than slaveholders at the south?

[Metcalf] I presume she did. I have heard her say so.

[Session] Did you know Miss Kelly to have a pledge?

[Metcalf] Yes I have seen it, but not that day. I never signed it.

[Session] Had you have any objection to signing it?

[Metcalf] I thought I could not sign it & maintain my connection with the church.

[Session] Did the pledge require the individual signing it not to fellowship any member of the church at the north who was any way connected with the church at the south?

[Metcalf] It required them not to support any pro Slavery churches or clergymen.

[Session] What do you understand by Pro Slavery?

[Metcalf] It means those connected with Slavery.

[Session] Did the pledge bind those signing it in case of insurrection of the slaves at the south that they should not help to put it down?

[Metcalf] I believe there was something of that kind in it.

[Gridley] By Mod.: Did you understand that pledge as inviting members of churches here at the north to come out & cease fellowship with their Brethren?[14]

[Metcalf] I so understand it to be so.

[Bement] By Defendant: Do you know whether Mrs. Bement signed that pledge?

[Metcalf] I do not.

Read to witness & approved.

---

[14]Northern ultraists often sought to separate from their southern coreligionists as a way of removing any taint of sin from their denominations. In 1844 the northern and southern Methodist churches split over the slavery issue. At about the same time, and for much the same reasons, the Southern Baptist Convention was founded. The Presbyterian Church did not formally divide on the issue of slavery until after secession, but the "Old School–New School" division of 1837 clearly had sectional overtones. Lutherans, Episcopalians, and Roman Catholics did not split until secession, although each had large constituencies in both regions.

[Judicatory]   Jabez Matthews sworn: Was you present at the Lecture of Miss Kelly on 1st Sabbath of August?

[Matthews]   I was present at a meeting on the Sabbath. Don't know what day of the month.

[Judicatory]   Do you consider that to have been a Moral & Religious Meeting?

[Matthews]   Yes I did.

[Judicatory]   Was there any portion of the Scripture read?

[Matthews]   There was one chapter.

[Judicatory]   Was there singing?

[Matthews]   Yes sir.

[Judicatory]   What was the character of the Hymn sung?

[Matthews]   It was Religious & Moral.

[Judicatory]   Have you that composition with you?

[Matthews]   Yes sir. Presented.

[Judicatory]   Was prayer offered either silent or otherwise?

[Matthews]   I thought there was silent prayer offered there.

[Judicatory]   Was it your impression from the language of Miss Kelly that she intended a short season of prayer then?

[Matthews]   I did.

[Gridley]   Moderator: Do you think if that meeting had been called for devotional & Religious worship that all professors that were there would have refused to open the meeting with Prayer?

[Matthews]   Perhaps so, if not called upon Personally.

[Gridley]   Whether he as a Presbyterian considered it proper for a female to call a promiscuous meeting for the purpose of addressing them on Moral & Religious subjects?

[Matthews]   I do.

[Gridley]   Does that coincide with the sentiments of the Presbyterian Church as manifested in their Religious worship in their usual manner of conducting their meeting?

[Matthews]   I believe not.

[Gridley]   Is it not the duty of a member of the Presbyterian Church to regard that sentiment, as in relation to his Brethren of the church to which he belongs, in his practice?

[Matthews]   I do not consider them under obligation. Do not think it is when they dipart [*sic*] from the rules of the Bible.

[Gridley]   Is the convenant with which members of the church enter with one another binding & ought to be regarded?

[Matthews]   Yes, so far as it agrees with the Bible.

[Gridley]   Is the duty of females to address promiscuous assemblies on Moral & Religious subjects so clearly established in the Bible as to justify members in going to hear them contrary to the established sentiment of the church to which they belong?

[Matthews]   I believe it is.

Read to Witness & approved.

[Judicatory]   Thos. J. Paine sworn: Do you believe in the Religion of the Bible?

[Paine]   Most heartily & decidedly.

[Judicatory]   Was you present at the Lecture of Miss Kelly 1st Sunday of August last?

[Paine]   I was.

[Judicatory]   How did you consider that, a Moral & Religious Lecture or not?

[Paine]   I considered it a Religious Lecture.

[Judicatory]   Was there reading of the Scripture? [Was there] what you call prayer & singing?

[Paine]   There was reading of scripture. There was a pause for some cause. I do not recollect any singing.

[Paine]   Here Witness requested to state that the Lecture was purely Religious but there were afterwards some remarks of a severe character.

[Judicatory]   During this Lecture did you discover anything that was improper for a professor of Religion to be present?

[Paine]   I did not.

[Session]   By Session: Was there a motion put at the close of the Lecture?

[Paine]   There was an expression of the sense of the meeting taken, approbating the sentiment advanced. It seemed pretty unanimous.

[Session]   What followed after the vote was taken?

[Paine]   She seemed to ask for the cooperation of the church to go with her in this enterprize & enquired where are your clergymen? Where is your Bogue? She thought he would burn her if he had it in his power & added she knew him [and] knew something about him.

[Session]   Do you think on the whole, taken together, that that was the kind of meeting that Christians could approve of?

[Paine]   Yes sir. The latter part I objected to.

[Gridley]   By Mod.: Would you consider that if a minister of the gospel should append to a very good lecture such remarks as Miss Kelly made use of would [he] be regarded as a safe Religious guide?

[Paine]   No sir I should not approve of it & I did not in her. I considered it very injudicious.

[Bement]   By Defendant: When she asked for your Bogue did she do it with disrespect to Mr. Bogue?

[Paine]   I considered she held him in very low estimation.

Read to Witness & approved.

[Judicatory]   Mrs. Bascom sworn: Are you a member of a Christian Church?

[Bascom]   I am a member of the Episcopal Church.[15]

[Judicatory]   Was you present at a lecture of Miss Kelly in August?

[Bascom]   I was seting in a window of our house & she was in our yard. I could hear Miss Kelly.

[Judicatory]   Did you consider it of a Moral & Religious character?

[Bascom]   I did.

[Judicatory]   Can you tell what she said of Mr. Bogue?

[Bascom]   I heard his name mentioned but my attention was called away.

[15]Trinity Episcopal Church was organized January 13, 1831.

[Judicatory]   Did you discover anything in the manner of Miss Kelly in that Lecture in which it was improper for a professor of Religion to be present?

[Bascom]   I did not.

[Session]   By Session: Do you know whether Mrs. Bement signed the Pledge?

[Bascom]   I do not.

Read to witness & approved.

[Judicatory]   Thomas Van Allstyne sworn: Are you a member of this church?

[Van Alstyne]   I am.

[Judicatory]   Did you attend a Lecture of Miss Kelly 1st of August last?

[Van Alstyne]   I attended one of them, I believe on that day.

[Judicatory]   Did you consider it of a Moral & Religious character?

[Van Alstyne]   I did, as good as I had heard for several years.

[Judicatory]   Did you discover anything in word or manner of Miss Kelly in that Lecture in which it was improper for a professor of Religion to be present?

[Van Alstyne]   I did not untill after the Lecture.

[Judicatory]   Did the Lecture change your views on the subject of American slavery?

[Van Alstyne]   It did. Previous to that time I supposed the Bible upheld American Slavery.

[Session]   By Session: What portion of the Bible was it you supposed upheld Slavery?

[Van Alstyne]   Ans.: The Old Testament.

[Session]   After the Lecture did you hear the churches of the North denounced?

[Van Alstyne]   I heard this church denounced, that she had been informed it was now bared [*sic*] against Antislavery, Temperance & Moral Reform and that Christians ought to be industrious in all good works.

[Session]   Did she charge upon any church or churches as being stealers of children?

[Van Alstyne]   She charged them as being in connection with man stealers, stealing women & children, & went on to explain, & did not mean to include all the members. For she believed there were some of them Honest.

[Session]   Did she connect the churches at the North with those at the South, and say they at the North were more guilty than at the South?

[Van Alstyne]   I did not so understand her. She said they were all connected & were equally guilty.

[Gridley]   By Moderator: Did Miss Kelly have a pledge which was presented to you?

[Van Alstyne]   No sir. But I understand she had a pledge.

[Gridley]   Did you hear Miss Kelly at that time say anything in relation to Mr. Bogue?

[Van Alstyne]   She said, there's your Mr. Bogue, & said, according to his principles he would stand & see her Burned at the stake. Said she knew him & his Father. Believed he was of a persecuting disposition and thought him not too good to see her burned at the stake.

[Session]   By Session: Was there a motion put & vote taken?

[Van Alstyne]   There was, but there was several amendments made & what the result was I do not know.

[Session]   Was there an uproar and considerable disturbance?

[Van Alstyne]   There was considerable talking & Miss Kelly requested they would be as still as possible for it was the Sabbath.

[Session]   Did that talking arise from some dissenting to what Miss Kelly had said?

[Van Alstyne]   No Sir, it appeared to be discussions about the Lecture, comparing it with scriptures etc.

[Session]   Did individuals take exception to what Miss Kelly had said, it not agreeing with the Bible?

[Van Alstyne]   I did not hear them.

Read to witness & approved.

[Bement] By Defendant: Mrs. Lum called again. What was Miss Kelly's expression in reference to Mr. Bogue?

[Lum] Ans.: She spoke about Mr. Bogue & said, I happen to know something about your Mr. Bogue, and his abolition principles, & by [about] his connexions with the southern churches, & [he] would approve of what Doctor Plumber[16] had said & would see her Burned or murdered as abolitionists had been at the south.

Read to witness & approved.

[Bement] By Defendant. Mrs. Perry sworn: Can you tell what Miss Kelly said about Mr. Bogue?

[Perry] Ans.: I would corroborate Mrs. Lum's testimony on that point.

[Bement] Was that the first Abolition Lecture you ever attended?

[Perry] Ans.: It was.

[Bement] Were your views on the subject of American Slavery changed by attendance on that Lecture?

[Perry] They were.

[Bement] What had been your views respecting American Slavery from the Bible?

[Perry] I never thought much about it. Our ministers had never told us anything about it & I had supposed there was no very great sin in it.

[Bement] Do you think you have received light from attending that Lecture?

[Perry] I think I did receive light.

[Bement] Where did the light come from?

[Perry] I think from above.

Read to Witness & approved.

[16]Miss Kelley was evidently referring to the Reverend William Swan Plumer (1802–1880), a Presbyterian clergyman who served as the pastor of the First Presbyterian Church, Richmond, Virginia. When the New School–Old School controversy split the American Presbyterian Church in 1837, Plumer led the Old School forces and a year later became moderator of the Old School General Assembly. While pastor in Richmond, Plumer founded and edited a religious and proslavery paper, the *Watchman of the South.*

[Judicatory]   Mr. Denison sworn: Can you tell us what Miss Kelly said respecting Mr. Bogue?

[Denison]   Miss Kelly had been endeavoring to establish the fact that the same persecuting spirit existed now that did in former ages, and that the proslavery persecutions was of that character. And [she] quoted what Mr. Plumber had said, that if abolitionists would set the country in a blaze it was but fair that they should take the first warning at the fire. And she asked, do you not believe that Mr. Bogue would burn her if he could and is he not in full fellowship with them and does he not endorse all they say?

[Judicatory]   Do you corroborate other witnesses as regards the Moral & Religious character of that meeting?

[Denison]   I do.

It is admitted by Defense that witness is Brother to the accused.

Read to witness & approved.

Adjourned to morrow 9 o'clock A.M.

Closed with Prayer.

Session met on adjournment.

Present as before.   Opened by Prayer.

[Brown]   Defense offer to introduce the Record of the session of this church to show that there has been no labour with Mrs. Bement on any of the specifications excepting the 3rd.[17] Over ruled by Moderator.

[Session]   Session. Mr. Matthews recalled: Did you attend other Lectures of Miss Kelly than the one spoken of?

[Matthews]   I did, two or three.

[Session]   What was the character of those Lectures which you attended?

---

[17]Mrs. Bement's argument, that because her accusers had not "labored" with her they had no right to bring charges against her, was technically correct, but it obviously did not impress the moderator.

[Matthews] They were attended with more propriety than some of our Religious meetings in this village.

[Session] Did you hear at any of those meetings the Rev. Doctor Richards[18] denounced?

[Matthews] I cannot say that I heard Miss Kelly do so, but I have heard his name mentioned by some one.

[Session] Did you hear her denounce this church?

[Matthews] Ans.: No more than other churches. She mentioned that this House was bared [*sic*] against Abolition, Temperance & Moral Reform Lectures.

[Session] Did you hear Miss Kelly make the charge against the northern churches, that they were guilty of stealing men, women & children?

[Matthews] I think she said they were all connected; that the Northern churches upheld the southern churches in robbing cradles.

Read to Witness & approved.

Defense now calls for Witnesses on 1st Specification.

[Judicatory] Thomas Van Allstyne sworn: What effect does the wine produce on you when you partake of it?

[Van Alstyne] Ans.: When it is poured out I smell it & when I take it, it produces heat in my face, either the smell or drinking of it.

[Judicatory] Do you suppose it produces any injurious effects on you?

[Van Alstyne] Ans.: It produces an inflammatory heat in my face.

---

[18]Miss Kelley probably talked about the Reverend Dr. James Richards (1793–1843), whose death on August 2, 1843, may have occasioned her comment. Appointed professor of theology at the Auburn Theological Seminary in 1823, Richards traveled extensively throughout New York State in an effort to raise money for the infant seminary. An opponent of revivalism, which he regarded as a spurious excitement, Richards also deplored the split of the Presbyterian church in 1837. Kelley undoubtedly was critical of Richard's contacts with Old School Presbyterian apologists for slavery. Coincidentally, Samuel H. Gridley, the moderator at Rhoda Bement's trial, wrote a biography of Richards in 1846; it is doubtful that he was at all sympathetic to Kelley's criticism of Richards.

[Session]   By the Session: What distance do you sit from where the Element is poured out?

[Van Alstyne]   I sit about two thirds the way back, not much over of 25 or 30 feet back.

[Platt]   By complainant: Do you profess to be judge of wine?

[Van Alstyne]   I can tell good from poor wine.

[Bement]   By Defendant: What is your opinion of the wine used in this church?

[Van Alstyne]   I supposed it to be as good as could be produced, though I judged it to be stronger than it had been proved to be.

Read to witness & approved.

3rd Specification

Defense here offer objections to investigating this specification:

1st There is no offense charged contrary to the word of God (see Book, page 391, Chapr. 1st, Sec. 3 & 4).[19] Charged simply with behavior towards Mr. Bogue & that kind of behavior not stated. If the charge of unchristian behavior be in the general charge, that does not remove the necessity of specifying particularly what that behavior consisted in. There is nothing in the specification implying sin, & cannot be amended by the general charge.

2nd objection: If it is an offense, it is a private offense & the necessary steps have not been taken & proof offered to substantiate the fact.

Objections over ruled.

[Platt]   By complainant. Hugh McAlister Jr. sworn: What conversation did you hear between Mrs. Bement & Mr. Bogue

[19]"An offense is anything in the principles or practice of a Church member, which is contrary to the word of God; or which, if it is not in its own nature sinful, may attempt others to sin, or mar their spiritual edification."
Section 4: "Nothing, therefore, ought to be considered by any judicatory as an offense, or admitted as matter of accusation, which cannot be proved to be such from Scripture, or from the regulations and practice of the church, founded on Scripture; and does not involve those evils, which discipline is intended to prevent" (*The Constitution of the Presbyterian Church*, p. 391).

in the vestibule of this church on the first Sunday of October last?

[McAlister] Mr. Bogue & myself were conversing in the vestibule of the church. Mrs. Bement came forward to Mr. Bogue and said to him: Why did you refuse to read my notice? Mr. Bogue's reply was: I saw no notice, Mrs. Bement. You must have seen it Mr. Bogue. I did not see it untill I dismissed the congregation. Mrs. Bement: I don't see how it can be possible you did not see it, for you are in the habit of reading notices left in the desk. Mr. Bogue repeated as before & said: I did not see it untill I had dismissed the congregation & God is my witness. Mrs. Bement I think replied again: I do not see how it is possible you did not see it. She went further I think and said: Mr. Bogue, I have reason to believe you are dishonest, it is my impression she added in this business. Mr. Bogue said to her: Mrs. Bement, I think the manner you pounce upon me is unchristian and unladylike. She said: I think differently. I think I have a right to put notices in the desk & have them read. I sent a notice to the desk last Sabbath. You refused to read it and called a meeting of session the next day to consult on it. Mr. Bogue replied: Mrs. Bement, you are mistaken in this whole matter & ought to be better informed before you make such charges. Mrs. Bement told Mr. Bogue that he had told her that he was an abolitionist.

[Session] By the Session: Did Mr. Bogue start to go out & was called back?

[McAlister] Yes sir. I think that was previous to Mrs. Bement's charging him with dishonesty.

[Brown] By defense: What reply did you make to Mrs. Bement? Objected to.

[Brown] Was it not in reference to the visit of Mr. Bogue & Doctor Brown to her Husband in which she used the words dishonest?

[McAlister] I understood it to be in connection with the notices & that visit both.

[Brown]   Did Mrs. Bement say to Mr. Bogue: Is it not your practice when you see papers on your desk to open them & see if they are proper to be read?

[McAlister]   I think she did.

[Brown]   Can you tell what Mr. Bogue said which lead Mrs. Bement to ask Mr. Bogue that question?

[McAlister]   She seemed to dispute Mr. Bogue's veracity in regard to the paper which he said he did not see untill after he had dismissed the congregation.

[Brown]   Did you in that conversation understand Mr. Bogue to say that he saw a paper on the desk before he dismissed the congregation?

[McAlister]   I think not.

[Gridley]   By Mod.: Did you regard this as a public transaction?[20]

[McAlister]   I do not know how to define the word public. If there being 10 or a dozen present made it public, it was public.

[Gridley]   Did Mr. Bogue demean himself as a Christian & a minister ought under the like circumstances?

[McAlister]   So far as I could judge he did.

[Gridley]   Did not Mrs. Bement seem to demean herself as a Christian, excepting as to the language?

[McAlister]   Yes sir, I think she did.

[Gridley]   What number should you think heard the conversation?

[McAlister]   I should think between 10 & 20 names. Stephen Easton, Mrs. Mark Squires, Miss Betsy Squires. [And] wit-

---

[20]According to the Book of Discipline, Chapter III, Section II (*The Constitution of the Presbyterian Church*, p. 393), a public offense occurs "when an offense is either so notorious and scandalous, as that no private steps would obviate its injurious effects; or when, though originally known to one, or a few, the private steps have been ineffectual, and there is, obviously, no way of removing the offense, but by means of a judicial process." Bement's accusers were thus at pains to prove that hers was a public offense, because in such cases private labors "are not necessary; but the proper judicatory is bound to take immediate cognizance of the affair."

nesses cited Miss Dumont, Mr. James Squires, 2 Ladies with Mrs. Bement.

[Brown] By Defense: Was this on communion day?

[McAlister] Yes.

[Session] By Session: Did Mrs. Bement give as her reason for doubting his veracity that she had sent in a notice the Sunday previous & that day she had put another in the Desk?

[McAlister] I cannot remember.

[Session] Did Mr. Bogue say: Mrs. Bement you seem to doubt my veracity?

[McAlister] Yes, I believe there was such conversation.

[Session] When Mr. Bogue said to Mrs. Bement, you seem to doubt my veracity, did she convey the impression to the witness that she did doubt it?

[McAlister] She did.

[Brown] By Defense: Have you and Mr. Bogue talked over this subject since the transaction?

[McAlister] We have talked on the subject several times.

Read to witness & approved.

[Judicatory] Syrine Edwards sworn: Was you present on 1st Sabbath of October last in the vestibule of the church at a conversation between Mr. Bogue & Mrs. Bement?

[Edwards] As Mr. Bogue wished all should take notice of it, I made a memorandum ([clerk's note] see page 177 which should come in here being the commencement of the testimony).

[Session] By Session: Do you know anything about that first notice which was handed to Mr. Pool?

[Edwards] Mr. Pool came to me during intermission & said he had a notice for an Abby Kelly Lecture and asked what he should do with it.

[Edwards] I saw Mr. Pool hand it to Mr. McAlister & he tore it up.

[Brown]   By Defense: Did you or did you not hear Mr. Bogue
say he saw the paper before he dismissed congregation?

[Edwards]   Not untill the Benediction, or before the congregation was dismissed.

[Brown]   Have you had conversation with Mr. Bogue on this
subject since that time?

[Edwards]   The next morning I met Mr. Bogue & laughed at
him some & he said I hope you will remember. I was once
since in Mr. Bogue's [house]. I laughed at him & told him
that Mrs. Bement had done to him as he had said they
ought when we had anything against a Brother. Mr. Bogue
said he did not tell them to do as she had done.

[Brown]   Did Mr. Bogue say she had done wrong & ought to
be punished?

[Edwards]   He said she had done wrong & should be punished. If he had any control in this Session she should not
go unpunished.

[Brown]   Was this in conversation with Mrs. Bement or after
they had separated?

[Edwards]   Mr. Bogue was not replying to Mrs. Bement.

[Brown]   Was this on communion day?

[Edwards]   Ans.: Yes.

[Brown]   What reason had you to think that Mrs. Bement
would not be to church in the afternoon?

[Edwards]   I thought Mrs. Bement would be ashamed to show
her face.

[Gridley]   By Mod.: How many persons should you think present at the time?

[Edwards]   I should think more than 4 or 5.

[Gridley]   Was this immediately after the morning service?

[Edwards]   Yes.

[Gridley]   Did Mr. Bogue demean himself as a Christian minister ought under such circumstances?

[Edwards]   I thought so.

[Gridley]   Was there anything in the demeanor of Mrs. Bement out of the way except the language?

[Edwards]   She was remarkably mild and decided.
[Session]   By Session: Do you think there might be 6 or 8?
[Edwards]   Yes there might be.
                              Read to witness & approved.

Testimony of Sering W. Edwards, read by him to the Judicatory—([clerk's note] and should have been entered as preceed-
ing his testimony by question & answer—see page 175).
[Edwards]   On communion day of last October, while I was
   standing on the porch I heard some persons talking in the
   hall, heard Mr. Bogue reply to Mrs. Bement but was not
   near enough to understand. Mrs. Bement says, why did
   you not read my notices. Mr. Bogue says, Madam I have
   not seen your notices—or I did not know anything about
   your notices untill this—think the last was the reply. Mrs.
   Bement says, you must have known about them. Mr. Bogue
   says, Madam you are mistaken. Mrs. Bement says, you certainly must have known about them for one was sent or
   passed to Mr. Poole last Sabbath to hand to you & I laid
   one on the desk this morning myself. Mr. Bogue says, I did
   not or don't know anything about any notice last Sabbath
   & why I did not see the one on the desk before I did, I
   cannot tell, but I did not know what it was untill the congregation was dismissed. [And] then I saw it lie there &
   picked it up, looked at it & saw what it was, but did not
   know where it came from for there was no name nor date.
   Mrs. Bement says, Mr. Bogue I think you are not honest in
   this matter for you could not help but know it & Mr. Bogue
   I think you are dishonest in this matter. Mr. Bogue says,
   Madam you are mistaken in this matter & it is not very
   polite in you to say so & you had better inform yourself
   better about it before you say so. Mrs. Bement says, I am
   not mistaken. Mr. Bogue says, how do you know you are
   not mistaken? Mrs. Bement says, because you called your
   session together Monday or Tuesday of last week for that
   purpose. Mr. Bogue says, Madam, I did not, for I did not

know anything about your notice. Mrs. Bement says, you did & you are dishonest. Bogue says, then you say that I am dishonest do you? Mrs. Bement says, yes I do. Mr. Bogue says, I want you all to take notice & says to Mrs. Bement, how do you know that? Mrs. Bement says, because you called your session together & sent Dr. Brown & some other person to confer with my husband. Mr. Bogue says, Madam that was not the business at all, & I did not know anything about your notice last sabbath there, and why I did not see the one to day I cannot tell, as I said before.

[Brown]   By Defense. Miss L. Denison sworn: Was you present at the conversation between Mr. Bogue & Mrs. Bement?

[Denison]   I was. I could not hear what Mrs. Bement said, except one question put by Mrs. Bement to Mr. Bogue.

[Brown]   What was that question?

[Denison]   If it was not his practice when he see papers lying upon the Desk, to read them?

[Brown]   Did Mr. Bogue admit he saw the paper lying there but did not open it untill after he had dismissed the congregation?

[Denison]   Yes, he said he saw it but did not open it.

[Brown]   Will you relate the conversation?

[Denison]   I cannot, for I could not hear what Mrs. Bement said, although I stood nearer than anyone else.

[Brown]   Did Mrs. Bement in that conversation speak louder than in ordinary conversation?

[Denison]   I think not.

[Session]   By Session: Are you a daughter of Mr. Denison who was sworn here yesterday?

[Denison]   Yes sir.

[Gridley]   By Mod.: Was your attention directed to the conversation?

[Denison]   It was not directly. [I was] not paying particular attention.

Read to witness & approved.

[Judicatory]   Mr. Vail sworn: Did you see Mrs. Bement lay a paper on the desk the 1st Sabbath of October last?

[Vail]   I saw Mrs. Bement lay a paper on the desk.

4th Specification:

[Hood]   C. Hood sworn: Mrs. Bement was not in her seat on the 1st Sabbath of October in the afternoon.

[Brown]   By Defense: Do you know of any reason why Mrs. Bement was not there?

[Hood]   I understood from Mrs. Bement that she thought she could not, under the circumstances, conscientiously attend.

[Brown]   Do you know any reason why she was not there?

[Hood]   It appears she spoke to Mr. Bogue on the subject of the papers & had not the difficulty removed in her mind at that time. She spoke to Mr. Bogue in relation to the papers, but the result was not satisfactory & she could not conscientiously attend the communion service.

[Brown]   Did she state to you the reason why she called on Mr. Bogue at the time she did?

[Hood]   That she might have the difficulty removed.

[Brown]   Did she also state that this was the only convenient opportunity she had to speak to Mr. Bogue?

[Hood]   I believe she did.

[Brown]   Did you understand from Mrs. Bement that she absented herself because Mr. Bogue did not read the notices?

[Hood]   It was because of Mr. Bogue's not reading the notices, Doctor Brown & Mr. Bogue visiting her Husband, & the conversation had between him & Mr. Bogue.

Read to witness & approved.

5th Specification:

[Bellows]   M. B. Bellows sworn: I returned, I believe, from Michigan 10th October. I think I have not seen Mrs. Bement at church when Mr. Bogue officiated since.

[Brown]   By Defense: Have you been regular in your attendance at church?

[Bellows]   I believe I have not been absent but 1 or 2 sabbaths.
[Brown]   Is it probable she should be at church and you not have seen her?
[Bellows]   I think not, for I have generally thought of it.
[Brown]   Do you know whether Mrs. Bement has been sick since?
[Bellows]   I do not.
[Brown]   Have you seen Mrs. Bement at any time since at church?
[Bellows]   I think I have once, I believe, when Mr. Gray officiated.
[Brown]   Have you ever since seen her here when Mr. Bogue officiated?
[Bellows]   I have not to my recollection.

                              Read to witness & approved.

[Judicatory]   J. K. Brown sworn: Tell what you know about Mrs. Bement being at church when Mr. Bogue officiated.
[Brown]   I do not know of Mrs. Bement's being present at any meeting when Mr. Bogue officiated. I have looked once.
[Session]   By Session: Would you not have known if Mrs. Bement had been there?
[Brown]   I think I should for some portion of the time, for I was on the watch, hoping to have met her in church.

                              Read to witness & approved.

[Judicatory]   Wm. Arnett sworn: Do you know anything with regard to the first notice of a Lecture of Miss Kelly?
[Arnett]   I saw a notice in the hands of the sexton. He said it came from a Lady, he did not know her. I desired him to see some other one of the Trustees [and] directed him to Mr. King. I directed him not to hand it to the Pastor without seeing some other one of the trustees.

                              Read to witness & approved.

[Judicatory]   Mrs. Lum called: Have you ever heard Miss Kelly say anything in regard to Rev. Doct. Richards?

[Lum]   I think I have. Cannot recall distinctly. It was some two or three years since. I cannot repeat the Language.

[Judicatory]   Did she severly denounce him?

[Lum]   I do not remember. I do not remember what her Language was. She assumed the fact that Doct. Richards was a slave holder & went on to state his case. She regarded the tenure by which he held the slaves as much more censurable than I did.

> Read to witness & approved.
> Adjourned to morrow 9 o'clock A.M.
> Closed with Prayer.

Session Resumed.
Opened with Prayer.   Present as before.

[Gridley]   Miss F. Sackett recalled. By Mod.: Was this Lecture of which so much has been said of Miss Kelly at the same hour of a stated meeting at this House?

[Sackett]   I met the congregation going home when I returned from Miss Kelly's meeting.

[Gridley]   Was this meeting of the church notified at the close of the communion service?

[Sackett]   Ans.: I do not recollect.

[Gridley]   Have you ever seen a certain pledge of which something has been said?

[Sackett]   I have hear [sic] it read.

[Gridley]   Can you tell us the substance of it?

[Sackett]   I cannot. I thought it objectionable & thought I should not like to sign it.

[Gridley]   Did you regard that pledge, if you had signed it, as requiring you to withdraw your fellowship from this church?

[Sackett]   I thought I should be obliged to do so if I signed it.

[Session]   By Session: Who presented it to you?

[Sackett]   It was not presented. I heard it read.

[Session]   Was it at that meeting?

[Sackett]   I think not, but at another. I heard it read at a public meeting.

[Brown]   By Defense: Do you wish to be understood that a person signing the pledge would consider themselves bound to leave the church unless it was a proslavery [the clerk clearly meant antislavery] church?

[Sackett]   I do not know that I should.

[Gridley]   By Mod.: Do you consider that if you had signed that pledge, would you have been obliged to withdraw your connection from this church, irrespective of your own views of this church?

[Sackett]   I should not.

[Gridley]   What was your main objection to signing that pledge?

[Sackett]   I thought I would be bound to withdraw from the church & did not like to do so.

                            Read by witness & approved.

[Judicatory]   Mrs. Lum called: Will you state what you have heard Miss Kelly say or advise members of this church in regard to leaving it?

[Lum]   Ans.: She said, if you can remain in the church & do any good there, I should advise you to remain where you can do the most good.

[Judicatory]   Did you ever hear her say so in presence of Mrs. Bement?

[Lum]   Mrs. Bement was present.

[Judicatory]   Do you know of Miss Kelly ever soliciting any of her friends in this place to sign the pledge?

[Lum]   I did not.

[Gridley]   Moderator: Do you consider the pledge was only intended for those out of the church?

[Lum]   I considered it for all the same as a Temperance pledge.

[Gridley]   Did she convey the impression that in her public teaching that this Presbyterian Church or Presbyterian Church or Presbyterian Churches of the North were pro-slavery churches?

[Lum] I cannot tell what my impressions would have been if I had not known anything about it myself.

[Session] By Session: Was you at the Methodist Meeting House[21] when Miss Kelly lectured there?

[Lum] I was.

[Session] Did you hear any remarks respecting Doct. Richards?

[Lum] I heard his name mentioned I think, I am not certain. [I have] no recollection of his being charged as a man-stealer. She spoke of him as a slave holder. I know there was a good deal of interruption that evening.

[Judicatory] Miss L. Denison called: Have you ever heard Miss Kelly advise Mrs. Bement to remain in the church?

[Denison] Ans.: Yes I have.

[Judicatory] Have you ever heard her advise others to remain in this church?

[Denison] I have heard her advise Mr. Bement.

[Gridley] By Moderator: Have you ever seen the pledge which has been spoken of?

[Denison] Yes sir.

[Gridley] Do you think signing that pledge would have required members to have come out of the church?

[Denison] I should. She said if they thought they could do any good by remaining they had better remain.

[Session] By Session: What did you understand by Miss Kelly advising them to remain in the church?

[Denison] She said, that if they could do any good, to remain.

[Session] Was it her object in advising members to remain, for the glory of God?

[Denison] I presume it was.

Read to witness & approved.

[Session] By Session. Jonathan Metcalf called: Do you recollect hearing Miss Kelly denounce Doct. Richards?

[21]Although Methodists had been meeting in private residences in Seneca Falls since 1812, the Seneca Falls Society of the Methodist Episcopal Church was not incorporated until 1829.

[Metcalf] It was my impression that she did put Doct. Richards under the class of man stealers & quoted Mr. Wesley[22] & others to show that all slave holders were on a level with man stealers.

Read to witness & approved.

[Session] By Session. Thos. Van Alstyne: Did you hear Miss Kelly call this a proslavery church?

[Van Alstyne] Yes, she said all churches which shut their doors against abolition Lectures & preaching on the sin of Slavery were proslavery. She said she understood that this church was shut against them etc.

Read to witness & approved.

[Gridley] D. W. Forman sworn. By Mod.: Do you know that Mrs. Bement absented herself from the communion on the 1st Sabbath of October?

[Forman] She has admitted to me she was not present. I have no recollection of it myself. I understood it from her confession.

[Brown] By Defense: Did she state the reasons?

[Forman] She said she had felt agrieved at Mr. Bogue for not reading the notices she had handed up. I felt called upon to see him in order to [affect] a reconciliation according to the directions of the 5th of Matthew.[23] [And] she [said she] had been met in the manner which prevented the reconciliation she had sought. [And] that she [said she] did not feel herself at liberty to go forward under that state of things, believing that it was her duty that if she had ought against a Brother to have it removed before going to the commun-

[22]John Wesley was born in England in 1703. His experiences at Oxford University and later as an American missionary produced a spiritual crisis in the 1730s and led to the founding of Methodism. Wesley adopted a firm antislavery attitude as evidenced in a letter to William Wilberforce: "Go on in the name of God and the power of his might, till even American slavery, the vilest that ever saw the sun, shall vanish away before it" quoted in C. T. Winchester, *The Life of John Wesley* (New York, 1906), p. 262. Wesley died in London on March 2, 1791.

[23]The biblical text refers to the Sermon on the Mount in Matthew 5 and apparently verse 22: "But I say unto you, That whosoever is angry with his brother without a cause shall be in danger of the judgment."

ion. She stated too, the reasons why reconciliation did not take place.

[Brown]   By Defense: On 1ˢᵗ Specification: I want to know the effect of the wine on you received at the communion?

[Forman]   Since Doctor Brown took charge of the element, I have rarely taken the cup in my hands & taken a sip merely, & not a swallow, but that it has prodiced vertigo & on some occasions so much so as to be felt during the day. I still felt it my duty to take of the cup & have uniformly done so. I do not attribute this effect to the greater or less quantity of alcohol contained in the wine, but to something of the fumes of wine which produces that peculiar affect upon me. I believe I could drink 1/2 glass of coniack [*sic*] Brandy without it producing the effect that the smelling of good Madeira wine, such as most used & approved in this country, would produce. I have received the wine at communion in other places lately & I find it had the same effect the wine here has.

[Brown]   By Defense: What has been your advice to Mrs. Bement on this subject of omiting to receive the cup?

[Forman]   I told her not to wound her conscience.

[Session]   By Session: Has Mrs. Bement absented herself since the 1ˢᵗ of October from the services of this House when the acting Pastor officiated?

[Forman]   I cannot tell excepting from her admissions. She has told me she has absented herself. I have seen her here but do not know whether any other one officiated. The last Sabbath I believe she was not here. My attention was called to it.

[Session]   Was this congregation in worship at the time of Miss Kelly's Lecture which has been spoken of?

[Forman]   When I came to service they had assembled & were assembling at the Lecture, & when I went home from Meeting they were about dispersing.

[Brown]   By Defense: Give us the reason of Mrs. Bement for not attending church since the communion, 1ˢᵗ Sabbath of October.

137

[Forman]   In the same conversation alluded to in my examination on the 4th Specification, Mrs. Bement said that in as much as the reconciliation had not been effected with Mr. Bogue, she did not feel that she could be profited by attending upon his preaching while that difficulty remained. But that she had urged to have the matter between her and Mr. Bogue investigated speedily, so that she might enjoy the services of the sanctuary, and she alluded to the different instances in which she had urged it upon me as a member of the session.

Read to witness & approved.

[Brown]   By Defense. Mr. Hood called: Was you within hearing of the conversation between Mr. Bogue & Mrs. Bement?

[Hood]   I could hear what they said.

[Brown]   Did she talk any louder than usual?

[Hood]   I think not. I should think from her manner that she wished to make some inquiry of Mr. Bogue. I supposed it to be a private conversation.

[Brown]   Did Mr. Bogue speak in a quite [sic] tone or manner?

[Hood]   I do not remenber that he spoke loud.

[Gridley]   By Moderator: Have you reason to believe that a knowledge of this Transaction was soon spread through the congregation?

[Hood]   I think it was.

Read to witness & approved.

[Brown]   J. K. Brown called: In procuring this wine which has been so much talked about, I inquired about the price and made an objection that it could not be pure wine, & was told that the higher priced Madeira wine was generally brandied wine & if I wanted an article for communion that I had not best to get that article. I was told that the higher priced wine was not a criterion of the quality.

Read to witness & approved.

138

D. W. Forman's request to be excused from voting on the question of sustaining the charges in this case & in its onward progress.

Request refused.

Moderator then put the question separately on each specification whether the charges be sustained. On the roll being called on the 1st Specification it was unanimously sustained. Also on the 2nd Specification. On the 3rd Specification, the vote was unanimous excepting the vote of D. W. Forman who voted in the negative. Charges on the 4th and 5th Specification were sustained unanimously.

It was then resolved that a committee be appointed to visit Mrs. Bement for the purpose of seeing if Mrs. Bement could not be brought to see that she had erred & endeavor that she might be made to make such confession[24] or acknowledgment as would be satisfactory to the session. Rev. S. H. Gridley, M. B. Bellows & M. C. Deming were appointed such committee.

Adjourned untill Tuesday next at 2 o'clock P.M.

M. C. Deming Clerk P.T.   Closed with Prayer.

Tuesday Jany. 30, 1844   Session met on adjournment.
Opened with Prayer.
Present: S. H. Gridley, Mod., D. W. Forman, M. B. Bellows, C. Hood, Hugh McAlister, & M. C. Deming.

The committee appointed to visit Mrs. Bement and labour with her on the matter of her offense reported that they had visited her, & held a long conversation with her on the various Specifications under the general charge. [And they] endeavored to convince her of the character & the degree of the wrong which the specifications involved but had not obtained

[24]The church required sinners to repent and confess, to show "sorrow for [their] sins, to declare [their] repentance to those who are offended; who are thereupon to be reconciled to him, and in love to receive him." If the judicatory was satisfied "as to the reality of the repentance," they could restore the convicted sinner to the privileges of the church (*The Constitution of the Presbyterian Church*, p. 83).

evidence that she would be willing to make any confession of disorderly & unchristian conduct.

Mrs. Bement appeared, and the session having advised her that the charge of disorderly and unchristian conduct had been sustained & of the nature & degree of confession which it became her to make as contained in Doc. A,[25] enquired of her whether she was willing to make such confession. She replied: "I have but one thing to say, and proceeded to recite the following words, 'For if I be an offender or have committed any thing worthy of death I refuse not to die; but if there be none of these things whereof these accuse me, no man may deliver me unto them—I appeal not unto Caeser but unto God.'"

The accused having withdrawn, D. W. Forman here presented his dissent & protest. See document B.[26]

On Motion Resolved that a committee on the part of the session be raised to reply to said dissent and protest of D. W. Forman. On Motion.

Resolved that the Moderator S. H. Gridley and M. B. Bellows compose such committee.

On Motion Resolved that Mrs. Bement be suspended from the Communion of this Church untill she give evidence of repentance and return to duty.[27] Which resolution passed unanimously, excepting D. W. Forman, who voted in the negative.

Session voted a paper, as containing the substance what Mrs. Bement might properly adopt as an acknowledgment of her error. See Doc. A. On Motion.

Resolved that the Pastor of this church, announce the result of the action of the session in this case, to the church & congregation, as he may think proper.

Adjourned.   Closed with Prayer.

                                        M. C. Deming Clerk P.T.

[25]We have been unable to locate this document.

[26]We have been unable to locate this document.

[27]If Mrs. Bement continued to refuse to repent and confess she was liable to excommunication, or expulsion from the church. "The design of excommunication is, to operate upon the offender as a means of reclaiming him; to deliver the church from the scandal of his offense; and to inspire all with fear, by the examination of punishment" (*The Constitution of the Presbyterian Church*, p. 389).

PART THREE

Varieties of Religious Activity:
Conflict and Community
in the Churches of
the Burned-Over District

GLENN C. ALTSCHULER

The principled defiance of Rhoda Bement, who was excommunicated when the Session learned that she had begun to attend the Wesleyan Methodist Church, is the stuff of which novels are made: a strong-willed, articulate woman, not unlike Anne Hutchinson, confronts the resourceful and powerful minister of the Presbyterian Church in a village that in five years would host a historic Women's Rights Convention.[1] Yet, if plot and heroine are self-evidently clear to the would-be novelist, the significance of the confrontation remains a matter for historical interpretation. On one level the Bement trial seems to confirm a thesis of Whitney R. Cross's classic *The Burned-Over District* (1950). In seeking to explain the origins, nature, and consequences of evangelicalism in Western New York, Cross claimed that revivalism was ultimately divisive because it spawned "ultraists" who would accept no compromises with sin. They believed that evil in the world could be eradicated completely and immediately, that the duty of true Christians was to sunder connections with all wrongs and wrongdoers. Divisiveness and church schism, then, were "virtually inevitable" results of attitudes that expanded "the category

---

[1]Jeremy and Rhoda Bement were subscribers to the Women's Rights Convention of 1848. See "The Cowing Scrapbook," Seneca Falls Historical Society MSS, Seneca Falls, New York.

of sin far beyond its accustomed limits" and rendered the mores of the community "forever open to challenge and subject to revision." Ultraists and their opponents developed a Manichean view that subordinated harmony to ideological purity: "Both sides recognized the increasing rigidity of their classifications. Both felt that anyone not fully with them must be against them, and indulged in persecution complexes."[2]

Indeed, the church records of Seneca Falls provide abundant evidence for this thesis. Eighteen forty-three was a turbulent year for Methodists and Baptists, as well as for Presbyterians. Dissatisfied with the failure of the Methodist Church to sever its connections with southern slaveholding brethren, thirty-nine Seneca Falls Methodists withdrew to form the militantly anti-slavery Wesleyan Methodist Church. The Baptist Church, meanwhile, was stunned by the revelation that Minister E. R. Pinney was a Millerite. Eighty Baptists left to await the removal of the heretical minister; when Pinney left the church in anticipation of the end of the world he took fifty members of his congregation with him.

Such evidence amply documents the reality of divisiveness and schism, but it should not, I believe, permit us to forget that a powerful desire for unity and harmony also shaped the actions of Protestants in the churches of the Burned-Over District generally, and in the Seneca Falls Presbyterian Church in particular. This desire, it is important to note, was built into the very structure and ideology of the churches. The existence of splinter groups and the activities of reformers often served to remind church members of the fragility of their institution

[2]Whitney R. Cross, *The Burned-Over District, The Social and Intellectual History of Enthusiastic Religion in Western New York 1800–1850* (Ithaca, 1950), esp. pp. 81, 136, 208, 358. Two articles that examine the divisive thrust of revivalist ideology are David B. Davis, "The Emergence of Immediatism," *Mississippi Valley Historical Review* 49 (1962), pp. 209–230, and John L. Thomas, "Romantic Reform in America," *American Quarterly* 17 (1965), pp. 656–681. William McLoughlin has recently characterized the Second Great Awakening in the North as a challenge "to the older way of life at every turn, producing endless schisms and theological debates." *Revivals, Awakenings, and Reform* (Chicago, 1978), p. 137.

and of the necessity, however difficult, of maintaining unity. Conservative, moderate, and even ultraist church members knew that they were a small and often beleaguered minority in their villages and towns; revivalism had enabled them to extend Protestant norms by bringing more people under the umbrella of church discipline. The churches, as T. Scott Miyakawa has observed, provided formal organizations in a society accustomed to working within voluntary groups for common goals.[3] The fellowship of revivalism and subsequent church membership, moreover, sensitized Protestants to the values they shared, called them to accountability in upholding and extending those values, and provided a practical means of doing so. For those fired by their commitment to the complete and immediate eradication of sin, the task was all the more difficult. Who better than a zealous Christian soldier could understand the profound truth of Ralph Waldo Emerson: "Nothing stands between man and God, yet how persistent that nothing is." What was one to do when so many brothers and sisters were blind to the light of truth? How could their eyes be opened? For Rhoda Bement and hundreds of her counterparts in other Burned-Over District churches, such practical and urgent questions evoked a variety of responses. It is a mistake, I think, to assume that even those who could barely contain their millennialist or perfectionist expectations were always unwilling or incapable of practicing patience and Christian forebearance with their "misguided" brethren. Withdrawal, expulsion, and schism were often courts of last resort, frustrated admissions on both sides that persuasion and truth were no match for the satanic forces of ignorance and indifference. If ultraists gave up on lukewarm Christians, could they hope to influence non-Christians? Thus, ultraist rhetoric was often an ideal to strive for, and many church members were prepared to understand and even to forgive those who momentarily fell short of that ideal and

---

[3]See T. Scott Miyakawa, *Protestants and Pioneers: Individualism and Conformity on the American Frontier* (Chicago, 1964), and Donald Matthews, "The Second Great Awakening as an Organizing Process," *American Quarterly* 21 (1969), pp. 23–43.

redoubled their efforts to attain it. Even some ultraists, as we shall see, sought ways to prevent differences from ripening into permanent divisions because they shared with their brethren a sense of fallibility and interconnectedness—as well as a firm resolve to create harmonious Protestant communities.

Perhaps Cross and others have undervalued this pragmatic, inclusive side of church activity because they did not examine local sources such as the Bement trial transcript. Cross, for example, made excellent use of regional sources, such as Presbytery and Association reports and denominational newspapers, but did not utilize the session or minute books of individual churches. It is at this very level, I would argue, that the relationship between motivation, rhetoric, and action can best be observed. Dissension, schism, and secession are dramatic events that are easy to document. The desire for harmony and unity is often ignored, or dismissed as rhetoric, perhaps because when it works best it is invisible. In this essay I examine how the Burned-Over District churches worked, and why unity and harmony were such vital concerns. At the end of the essay I return to the Bement trial to show that ultraists and moderates came to a parting of the ways only with the utmost reluctance.

Although the conversion experience was a sudden, cataclysmic event in the life of a Christian—one that was often accompanied by a loss of bodily control—membership in the church was usually an orderly process that emphasized understanding of doctrine as much as faith. A resolution of the Session of the Presbyterian Church of Seneca Falls prescribed that application for membership must be made "at least four weeks previous to the communion at which they intend to unite with us." The Session ordered that in the interim the applicant receive instruction in "the doctrines of the Bible and in experimental religion." One or more members of the Session would visit the hopeful convert and make a report to the Session on lecture day.⁴ Methodists tested the conviction of converts by placing them on "probation" for an unspecified length of time. The ardor of those admitted at the instant of conversion, church officers recognized, often cooled as quickly as it had been ignited; the interval between conversion and admission provided the applicant an opportunity to test his or her faith. Church members hoped to avoid embarrassments, such as that experienced by Galen's First Baptist Church: William Brownell, baptized only two weeks earlier, was excluded when he used "vulgar and unbecoming language," and proclaimed that "his relation of his Christian experience before the church was wholly false." Transgressions, past and present, were also areas of legitimate inquiry by the Session. The discussion and resolution of a case before the Presbyterian Church of Romulus was typical: a husband and wife sought to join the church, but admitted to the crime of fornication. "The woman dates her conversion previously to committing the crime, the man since. The Session agreed to admit both people, if each made a confession, in public or in writing."⁵ Public confession was preferred by virtually all Burned-Over District churches because it permitted the congregation to reject sin, forgive the sinner, and coalesce around clearly articulated, common values.

Indeed, the standards for admission often required acknowledgment of and adherence to norms of preferred behavior. The Seneca Falls Presbyterian Church deemed it proper to ask an applicant if he or she does "practictly [*sic*] adopt the principle of entire abstinence from the use of ardent spirits except when necessary as a medicine."⁶ Significantly, this ultraist re-

⁴Session Minutes, First Presbyterian Church of Seneca Falls, May 14, 1834. Department of Manuscripts and University Archives, Cornell University, Ithaca, N.Y. (hereafter cited as M and UA, CU).
⁵Session Minutes, First Presbyterian Church of Romulus, August 18, 1807, September 4, 1807, M and UA, CU.
⁶Session Minutes, First Presbyterian Church of Seneca Falls, November 6, 1830, M and UA, CU. Other churches may have been reluctant to risk exclusions by setting down such strict requirements for membership. Not until August 21, 1858, did the Trumansburg Baptist Church resolve to refuse membership

quirement was not written at the height of revival enthusiasm but was passed by the Session shortly before the revival in 1831. Also, as we shall see, "entire abstinence" was not actually required of church members and, it is important to add, was never used to exclude a prospective Christian. Although seldom invoked, strict standards of admission were clearly useful in reminding Christians of their duty. Many converts must have understood one woman's request that the Session not receive her as planned, but that she remain under its care a while longer.[7] Presumably the crucible of doubt, introspection, and Christian tutelage produced stable, conscientious church members.

Church membership, then, carried with it the weighty responsibilities of Christian fellowship in towns plagued by temptation and sin. The denomination was an oasis in a desert of corruption; the convert was acutely aware that the vast majority of townspeople were without faith. I have found no communities where the combined Protestant denominational membership exceeded one-fourth of the total population, even at the height of Burned-Over District awakenings. Though the number of Protestants in Seneca Falls can only be estimated, an examination of membership rolls strongly suggests that no more than one quarter of the population had a denominational affiliation. The Presbyterian Church reported 197 members in 1843, and I have calculated the Baptist membership at 252[8] and the Methodist congregation at 330. These figures are almost certainly too high because they include every individual who joined the church and was not explicitly dismissed, withdrawn,

---

to those who engaged in cardplaying or dancing. Few were as strict as the Covert Baptist Church, which on September 8, 1810, required a unanimous vote of the congregation to receive a new member. Most churches acted by consensus, not votes.

[7]Session Minutes, First Presbyterian Church of West Fayette, May 7, 1825, M and UA, CU. The woman was unanimously received into the church the next day.

[8]Included in this number are the fifty people who left with Pinney and the eighty who stayed out of the church until a new minister arrived.

or excluded before 1843. Clerks often noted that a member was "gone," "dropped," or "removed by letter," but they did not always affix a date to the departure; I have counted all such people as church members. Many people, moreover, left town, stopped coming to church, or died, without the knowledge of the minister or clerk. The records of the Episcopal and Wesleyan Methodist churches, unfortunately, are fragmentary and my estimates are more appropriately labeled guesses. Since all acounts of the birth of the Seneca Falls Wesleyan Methodist Church indicate that it resulted from a secession from Methodists, I have assumed that all thirty-nine Methodists who withdrew in 1843 became Wesleyans and constituted a majority of the new church. It is extremely unlikely, then, that there were more than seventy-five Wesleyan Methodists in 1843. Finally, the presence of Seneca Falls's most prominent citizens as vestrymen testifies to the elite character of Trinity Episcopal Church. There were probably no more than 150 Episcopalians in Seneca Falls. Thus, no more than one thousand people claimed a Protestant denominational affiliation in Seneca Falls in 1843. In a township that recorded 4,281 inhabitants in 1840 and 4,053 people five years later, Protestants had good reason to feel that the Word had not reached the homes of many of their fellow townspeople.[9]

Fear of paganism, religious indifference, and Roman Catholicism gripped villages like Seneca Falls. Its proximity to the Erie Canal and its ample waterpower for manufacturing led to a rapid influx of various groups: natives and immigrants in search of land and work, brawling "canawlers," who were often Irish Catholic, canal boat gamblers, and prostitutes. In towns

[9]The census figures are undoubtedly too low because they do not reflect transients who lived in town in 1843 but left some time before the enumeration. Others, no doubt, arrived in Seneca Falls shortly after the enumeration. The proportion of Protestants to church members in Seneca Falls, it should be added, was far higher than the national average, which Winthrop Hudson estimates at 1:8 in 1835. See *Religion in America* (New York, 1965), p. 129. My point, however, is that Protestants quite properly viewed themselves as a minority and were therefore justifiably concerned with maintaining and augmenting their numbers.

containing great numbers of footloose wanderers, Christians could hardly decide where to begin the work of eradicating sin. No wonder a clergyman wrote despairingly to the American Home Missionary Society:

> There is great need here of a few more preserving men of infleuence, who will, through principle, give some attention to buildding up society. The want of this must render the labour of a minister in vain. He may concert the best plans, and try to do much for the welfare of souls, but the want of a few like Aaron . . . to stay up his hands, will render his plans abortive, and they must necessarily fail of being carried into effect.[10]

Revivals provided ministers with a few Aarons, but the church had to construct a strategy to bring Christian principles to still recalcitrant townspeople.

The first, the most indispensable and practicable step was to make certain that all church members lived as moral Christians. If converts had no power over many of their fellow citizens, they did feel responsible for those with whom they shared fellowship. Here was an opportunity to wrestle with Satan and to win. Two incidents are instructive. In 1832 the Seneca Falls Presbyterian Session investigated intemperance charges against John Brown. The defense sought to demonstrate that Brown was not drunk by asking witness James Gay: "Does he not usually act odd and singular?" Gay replied: "Don't know that he does. I took more notice the second or third time knowing that he was a member of the church." Tabor Potter's trial for using profane language evinced a similar sensitivity to the behavior of professing Christians. The Session clerk tartly recorded the testimony of William Sickels: "Witness had frequently heard previous to that time that Mr. Potter was a church member. Witness thinks if he had heard Mr. Potter use the language charged he should have noticed it and recolected [*sic*] it." Church members were evidently held to a higher code of conduct, and

---

[10]John Calvin Morgan to Rev. Miles Squier, April 25, 1827, American Home Missionary Society MSS, Amistad Research Center, New Orleans, La.

if conscience proved an unreliable guide the discipline of the church could be expected to call them to their duty.[11]

The methods by which frontier Presbyterians, Baptists, Methodists, and Quakers administered church discipline has been clearly described by T. Scott Miyakawa. Discipline procedures were remarkably similar in variety, range, and purpose. The key differences were structural rather than substantive: the autonomous Baptists tried cases before the whole church, the Presbyterian Session administered justice but permitted appeals to the Presbytery, and the Methodists worked through the class and, if necessary, the Quarterly Meeting. Miyakawa is surely right to say that discipline was the means by which the churches maintained "their group standards and unity," yet he does not, I think, fully take account of the dilemma of denominational churches in communities where a healthy majority were not professed Protestants. Recruits for Christ's army were hard to come by even in the Burned-Over District; suspension or excommunication, even of a few, imperiled the resources of the church. Withdrawal, even on matters of principle, carried great risk because it involved the loss of influence with one's brethren and sisters, and over church policy. If a "willingness to expel recalcitrant members when necessary" and "caution in accepting new members" suggest that frontier Baptists "were not interested in numbers as such,"[12] the more settled churches of western New York usually rejected such a Gideonite approach. Swept up in the "egalitarian revolution" of Jacksonian Era politics, they viewed numbers as palpable indications of the strength of the parties of Christ and Antichrist.

The delicate task of the churches, then, was to create a vital fellowship by insisting on Christian behavior, without thrusting

[11]Session Minutes, First Presbyterian Church of Seneca Falls, May 16, 1832, April 2, 1838, M and UA, CU.
[12]Miyakawa, *Protestants and Pioneers*, p. 39. Sidney Mead has suggested that "the revivalists' emphasis that Christ came to save sinners had the effect of encouraging the Church to nurture sinners in order that it might save them." See *The Lively Experiment: The Shaping of Christianity in America* (New York, 1963), p. 125.

the weak outside the denominational sphere of influence. Virtually all the churches in the Burned-Over District recognized that they must apply discipline sparingly and cautiously. Indeed, revival churches, with a few exceptions, used discipline little differently from institutions barely touched by enthusiasm. Most expulsions, ironically, stemmed from the churches' desire to include *more* people in communion. After an 1837 revival, the First Baptist Church of Newark, New York, sent a committee to visit members who had neglected church ordinances for an extended period of time. The hope, of course, was that these delinquent members could be persuaded to return to the church. The committee reported "favorable to all" except Josiah St. John and Jesse Brown, "who gave no encouragement to resume there [*sic*] travel." The promise of attendance, rather than the reality of attendance, it should be noted, was sufficient for the committee, which continued its investigation of St. John and Brown more for their attitudes than for their actions. St. John appeared before the church and explained that he did not attend ordinances because the church had neglected to heed his objection to an individual who had sought membership. Thus, "it was no privilege to him to belong to a church that would do Business in that way." St. John offered to pay his share of church expenses, but refused to pay "the average proportion" as assessed by a committee. The church patiently informed St. John that they "did not intend to treat him unkindly," although they insisted that they had "no remorse of conscience in the review in doing as they have in relation to him." After a month filled with "additional gospel steps," the Church sent an Epistle of Love to Brother St. John, who acknowledged his fault in neglecting church ordinances but stubbornly refused to pay his assessment. More than two months later he was excluded. The story, however, does not end in 1838 but in 1853 when, after many visits, a committee visited and then reclaimed St. John for the Baptist Church.[13]

[13]Minutes of the First Baptist Church of Newark, October 21, 1837, November 4, 1837, November 14, 1837, February 17, 1838, November 12, 1853, M and UA, CU.

Jesse Brown was equally troublesome. Brown admitted drinking "and had no determination to leave it off nor to make any confession in any way publicly." He had "no confidence in himself" and asked the church to set him aside. The committee labored further with Brown, who finally told them that he "dare not make any more promises and did not wish to make the church any further trouble." Still the church did not act until another month had elapsed, and when Brother Brown did not appear, they excluded him.[14] The reluctance of the Newark Baptist Church to expel its members was by no means atypical. By far the largest number of suspensions and excommunications were of individuals who had for years neglected ordinances and who, when labored with, rejected the hand of fellowship; only then did the churches acknowledge a fait accompli.

Some churches even refused to expel those who spurned them. John F. Cross told a committee of the Seneca Falls Baptist Church that he had no interest in religion, refused prayers, and expected and wished exclusion. The church deferred action pending further labors and two months later the committee reported that Cross now expressed interest in remaining in church, but did not enjoy religion and felt that he could not fellowship with the church. Even this tepid response did not discourage the committee, which labored for three more months to no avail. The church then discharged the committee, inexplicably dismissed the case, and John Cross disappears from the historian's view.[15] If the Seneca Falls Baptist Church had just one Cross to bear, the Presbyterian Church of Seneca Falls showed its unwillingness to expel a whole group of recalcitrant members. A committee sent to visit habitually negligent communicants in 1844 lamely refused to name names:

> As they have not the records before them they are not able to give a correct list and as it might seem invidious to select out of the members who are supposed to be faulty in the matter referred to

[14]Minutes of the First Baptist Church of Newark, December 4, 1837, January 5, 1838, February 17, 1838, M and UA, CU.

[15]Minutes of the First Baptist Church of Seneca Falls, February 23, 1841, April 27, 1841, July 13, 1841, M and UA, CU.

them and furthermore as some of those who are in the habit of
neglecting the ordinances of the church are aged, infirm or unable to procure conveyance—the Committee have thought it best
not to report the names of any, believing that this course will be
the most for edification, especially if followed as they hope it may
be by a course of kindness by individual members of Session towards any who are ascertained to have neglected the ordinances
and institutions of the church without sufficient cause.

The Session accepted this extraordinarily conciliatory report
without comment.[16]

The significance of discipline lay less in the actuality or even
the threat of censure or expulsion than in the maintenance of
the church's reputation and in the opportunity to reaffirm the
boundaries of permissible behavior. Hence the churches insisted on "private labors" and, if necessary, public confession.
Private labors permitted a church to settle disputes before they
became controversies, thereby preventing "injury to the prosperity of the church." The Baptist Church of Covert voted
that "every time the Church acts in Discipline or in any matters
of Difficulty it shall be in as private a manner from the world as
is possible."[17] This approach often bore fruit: the Geneva Methodist Church appointed a committee to labor with E. Silkerson
and wife, although no charges had been filed against them. The
committee called on the Silkersons, who "were not living hap-
pily together," and affected a reconciliation. So far as they could
tell, the matter was settled and "completely forgotten."[18]

Not all controversies, as our reading of the Bement trial in-

[16]Session Minutes, First Presbyterian Church of Seneca Falls, March 1, 1844,
M and UA, CU.
[17]Minutes of the Covert Baptist Church, May 17, 1805, M and UA, CU. This
resolution was reaffirmed on February 8, 1817.
[18]Leaders' Meeting of the Methodist Church of Geneva, April 18, 1836, M and
UA, CU. Although Methodist records are relatively scarce, perhaps because
itinerant ministers carried them away when they left town, church discipline
appears similar to that practiced by Baptists and Presbyterians. The Methodist
Church of Geneva had a mere handful of expulsions over a thirty year period. See also "Immorality Trials," Methodist Collections, Syracuse University,
Syracuse, N.Y.

dicates, could be so easily and amicably settled, yet churches sought to use disputes to reaffirm, to both members and outsiders, that they were bulwarks of moral probity. Church officials, for example, frequently viewed questionable business practices, even if technically legal, as breaches of discipline. The First Presbyterian Church of Lyons charged one communicant with dishonesty in buying a mortgage for 30 percent less than its face value, when the mortgage was considered good and safe. When the accused told the Session that his "time was too important to be spent in this way," he was suspended.[19] Not coincidentally a very substantial percentage of businessmen boasted denominational affiliation and wore it as a guarantee of their fairness.

Public confession also put the church's best face before the community, while facilitating the reclamation of wayward Christians. The confession was in a sense a mini-revival in which sinners rededicated themselves to a clearly delineated set of values. David Cook's confession of intemperance acknowledged the salutary effect suspension had had upon him: "I have taken a serious and I trust prayerful view of the subject and do believe I have reason to rejoice in such suspension as the means under God as I hope and believe bringing me to repentance and reformation."[20] Catherine Decker, "a woman of color," confessed to the sin of fornication but the Presbyterian Session of Geneva found her unrepentant and excommunicated her. Four years later she was restored when in her new confession she confirmed the earlier judgment of the Session:

> In the shame and confusion with which I was overwhelmed I did attempt by falsehood and prevarication to cover my sin and did

[19]Session Minutes, First Presbyterian Church of Lyons, August 12, 1844, September 24, 1844, October 12, 1844, M and UA, CU. On February 6, 1845, the suspension was changed to an admonition. In Galen's First Baptist Church (March 23, 1833, April 6, 1833), M and UA, CU, Brother Foster proclaimed "shit of the church if it would not allow him to collect his debts." The volatile Foster alternately conferred and then flew into a "violent passion"; eventually he was reconciled with the church and his debtors.
[20]Session Minutes, First Presbyterian Church of Geneva, January 27, 1825, M and UA, CU.

several times deny the crime of which I had been guilty. . . . I am anxiously desirous of being restored to the fellowship of the church . . . casting myself upon your charity and the mercy of God I remain your & c (signed by Mark).[21]

Decker's penitence enabled the church to practice Christian charity, and to establish itself as the moral vanguard of a sinful community.

The similarities in the application of discipline by revival and nonrevival churches highlight a fact often ignored by historians of the Burned-Over District. Church structures, practices, and traditions usually *preceded* revivalism and provided the context in which enthusiasm waxed or waned. The church officers, conscious that so many of their neighbors had no denominational affiliation, maintained a powerful centripetal force against the divisive tendencies of revival enthusiasts. Church elders usually served for life. They provided the continuity, the stability, and often the caution that anchored the churches against the winds of new doctrines, absolutist demands, and charismatic itinerants. We know that perfectionists, Millerites, and abolitionists sometimes split churches, but we must also remember, for example, that the First Presbyterian Church of Hector suspended fewer than one person per year, and experienced no secessions or conflicts over religious doctrine or reform activity. The search for consensus, in fact, often accelerated in revival churches: the First Baptist Church of Geneva voted in 1835 to retain Elder Sears, 34 yeas, 11 nays. Sears acknowledged the split; "under existing circumstances he thought it his duty to leave us." Another vote yielded an even larger majority to keep Sears, but the elder refused to minister to a divided church and asked for dismission.[22] If unity was the motivating force that initiated revivalism, that purpose may well have been reaffirmed with new force in the face of divisiveness.

[21]Session Minutes, First Presbyterian Church of Geneva, November 18, 1829, May 3, 1833, M and UA, CU.
[22]Minutes of the First Baptist Church of Geneva, December 13, 1835, December 20, 1835, January 2, 1836, March 5, 1836, M and UA, CU.

The transformation of revivalism from individual conversion to social reform, John L. Thomas has argued, unleashed "the very forces of secular perfectionism the conservatives most feared." Abolitionist crusades over alcohol and slavery, most historians agree, posed the greatest danger to church harmony. Indeed, evidence abounds to support this assertion. The Presbyterian Church in Rose, for example, split in two because, the insurgents explained, the church "suffers unrebuked one portion of her members to chattelize and traffic in the souls and bodies of another portion of her own members . . . annihilating the distinction which God has established between the nature and conditions of immortal man, and the beasts that perish." When the Rose church refused to hear testimony against slavery, secession resulted.[23] As I have indicated, both the Baptist and Methodist churches of Seneca Falls were by no means free from schism. Such conflict occurred more frequently in Burned-Over District churches than elsewhere, but it does not, I would maintain, constitute *the* logic of revivalism, nor *the* strategy inevitably pursued by ultraists. More often than not, benevolent efforts, accomplished through voluntarism and moral suasion, unified the church while providing a means of extending its influence over the larger social body. On many occasions, moreover, ultraists found ways to make their point without compromising their consciences or sundering their churches.

The cause of temperance is an important case in point. I have found no instance in which churches divided on the abstinence pledge. Yet if communicants agreed on the goal, they recognized as well the difficulty of attaining it, even among church members. The First Baptist Church of Trumansburg was typical: "The Temperance cause continues to meet the approbation of the Church, but we fear there is not that hearty cooperation among professors of Religion on this subject that

[23]Samuel Lyman, Gideon Henderson, Daniel Lovejoy, William Lovejoy to E. Flint, May 12, 1846, Wayne County Historical Society, Lyons, New York. See also James Gregg to Brethren of Rose Presbytery, March 11, 1850, and to the Presbytery of Geneva, Wayne County Historical Society, Lyons, New York.

there ought to be."[24] The *Water Bucket*, a Seneca Falls newspaper, acknowledged with regret that "the fact that many professing to be Christians are holding back from the work, is undeniable. We hope they have an excuse, which will satisfy the great judge of all the earth in the great day which shall try men's souls." Ultraist resolutions of total abstinence helped provide the denomination with a reputation for sobriety while establishing a standard of behavior for all communicants to emulate, but church elders recognized that perfect obedience could not be expected. A year after the Seneca Falls Presbyterian Church embraced "entire abstinence," Abel Downs admitted selling liquor to John Brown. When Downs realized that Brown was intoxicated, he averred, "we have since refused him [alcohol]."[25] The Session took no steps to discipline Abel Downs.

Voluntary pledges of temperance, Protestants quickly learned, provided an entering wedge into politics. More often than not they downplayed differences over such matters as the kind of wine to be served at communion (such disputes could best be left to individual consciences); the church, most agreed, must speak with one voice to the community. If "entire abstinence" served in part as a goal to which church members aspired, it also served as a strategy and rallying cry to make towns relatively more sober. Again and again church members demanded that the licenses of all taverns be revoked. Although unsuccessful in achieving their main goal, such petitions and remonstrances at least forced the Board of Trustees of the Village of Seneca Falls, for example, to make temperance an aim of local government:

Whereas the retail and use of intoxicating drinks is an evil productive of more misery, crime and poverty then all other causes combined, and directly or indirectly a greater tax upon the inhabitants of this village than all other taxes including all the com-

[24]Minutes of the First Baptist Church of Trumansburg, August 31, 1833, M and UA, CU.

[25]Session Minutes, First Presbyterian Church of Seneca Falls, May 16, 1830, M and UA, CU.

mon schools or the village, and whereas those engaged in the traffic are bound to the support of our public institutions, we now appeal to their general sentiments for we recognize among them many who are esteemed and respected as neighbors and friends to discontinue a practice so opposed to the interests of the tax-payers of this village, and in case of their refusal it is hereby resolved and we do hereby pledge ourselves to sustain the Best of the village in using all lawful means to suppress the same.[26]

Within a few years the board began to curtail the number of licenses granted, and church members could justly claim much of the credit. Temperance had surely become a "Protestant cru-sade" with the churches serving as the moral vanguard of the community.[27] Significantly, temperance became a divisive issue in many towns (though still not in the churches), when some insisted that coercion be substituted for voluntarism through passage of Maine Law legislation. This conflict, however, came long after the revival fires had cooled and may indeed have been a response to the decline of enthusiasm in the Burned-Over District.

The abolition of slavery provided different opportunities for Protestant churches—and different problems. Denunciations of slavery unified revival converts in towns that had no slaves and few, if any, blacks, by providing an opportunity to "bear wit-ness" to the immorality of bondage. Whitney Cross expressed it well: "Slavery presented a much more convenient challenge, for it did not have to do with the transgressions of friends and neighbors. It naturally seemed a far more enormous evil. . . . By comparison, temperance seemed nearly accomplished."[28]

[26]Minutes of the Board of Trustees of the Village of Senca Falls, May 5, 1840, Village Clerk's Office, Seneca Falls.

[27]The Village Minutes testify to the persistent and increasingly successful ef-forts of temperance advocates. See especially June 1, 1840, May 6, 1850, April 4, 1853, April 17, 1854, February 5, 1855, June 10, 1855.

[28]Cross, *The Burned-Over District*, p. 276. Interestingly the First Baptist Church of Geneva attempted to settle the problem of its black communicants pragmat-ically and with an appeal to voluntarism: "That those of the colored and white brethren who choose to sit together at Communion shall be permitted the privilege, and those of our white brethren who wish to sit by themselves the

159

Amid ardent interdenominational competition, abolitionism sometimes became the guidepost in determining which was the most morally pure church. Thus some churches denounced slavery with rhetorical extravagance, and experienced little or no dissension within the ranks.

Not all churches, to be sure, escaped conflict over abolitionism. Abby Kelley, as we have seen, toured the countryside with a pledge that bound its signers to condemn slavery as a sin, to demand immediate emancipation, and to cease fellowship with slaveholding coreligionists in the South. As Jan Saltzgaber has demonstrated, such agitators were particularly troublesome; they not only challenged the cautious approach that Protestant denominations took on the issue of slavery, but their very presence on public platforms raised the issue of women's proper role in a society accustomed to male domination.[29] The pitfalls of such activism were all too apparent to those who attended Kelley's lectures and watched the divisions in the Seneca Falls Methodist Church give birth to the Wesleyan Methodist Church. Regional and national schisms among Methodists, Baptists, and Presbyterians in the 1840s and 1850s can be attributed, directly or indirectly, to this issue. Such conflict, however, was not necessarily accompanied by the disintegration of individual churches. Some of the evidence for divisiveness involves secessions of whole churches from the Presbytery or Association, or shifts of entire congregations from Presbyterian to Congregational polity. Such actions were undoubtedly traumatic, but they often bound church members more closely together in the certainty of their convictions, while strengthening the influence of particular churches in the community.

I am suggesting, then, that the lines between ultraists and moderates were not always so rigidly drawn as Cross and others

---

same, with the proviso, that no slur be cast on either side, and if anyone does to be dealt with accordingly." Minutes of the First Baptist Church of Geneva, December 14, 1837, M and UA, CU.

[29]For the dilemma of ministers whose congregations were split on abolitionism see Donald H. Scott, *From Office to Profession: The New England Ministry, 1750–1850* (Camden, N.J., 1978), p. 104.

believed. The two groups were bound together by common goals, common enemies, and a recognition that the church was an important bulwark, indeed the only bulwark, against sin in communities where the majority of people had no institutional affiliation with Protestantism. They often agreed that the churches must be pragmatic and even at times tolerant of transgressors if they hoped to extend their influence. Differences were real and deeply felt, but they usually concerned means rather than ends. Schisms occurred all too frequently, but the divisive tendencies of Burned-Over District revivalism were moderated by a powerful centripetal counterforce that attracted and retained members while reaching out in an effort to create Protestant communities.

During the trial of Rhoda Bement virtually every issue that troubled Burned-Over District churches was joined. If abolition, temperance, and (perhaps indirectly) women's rights were on trial, so too was church unity. Tactics shaped the struggle between Mr. Bogue and Mrs. Bement just as surely as pride and principle did and, at least at the outset, neither protagonist appeared angry enough to try to divide the church or seriously weaken its authority.

At first Bogue and Bement were reluctant dragons, sometimes straining to avoid conflict. The minister certainly knew that several in his congregation had attended Abby Kelley's "exhibition," in which he had been denounced by name. He knew as well that they had neglected church services in favor of this abolitionist meeting. Yet Bogue did not act, probably with the hope and expectation that the hullaballoo would cease with the departure of the "outside agitator," Miss Kelley. Only when Mrs. Bement confronted him in the vestibule, with several people present, did the minister have charges brought against her. Here was a threat to ministerial authority, a danger especially acute to an acting pastor.[30] "If he had any control in this Ses-

[30]The number of temporary ministers increased dramatically during the first half of the nineteenth century. For the effect on ministers see Scott, pp. 120–121.

sion," Bogue was said to have promised, "she should not go unpunished."

If the initial restraint of Horace Bogue is to be expected of a minister and a moderate, the caution and patience of Rhoda Bement are more striking and surprising. Deeply moved by Kelley's "gospel lecture on the duty of Christians," she was doubtless disturbed by the attacks on her minister (who would see Kelley "burned at the stake" if he could) and by the pledge that disfellowshipped Presbyterians from slaveholders and apologists. Mrs. Bement burned to "bear witness" against slavery, but she was not sure how to do so. Two things seem certain: Rhoda Bement did not sign the pledge and she did not intend to leave the Seneca Falls Presbyterian Church. Both Eleanor Lum and Miss Dension testified, moreover, that Abby Kelley had advised people to stay in the church if they thought they could do good there. In fact, in the weeks between Miss Kelley's lecture and the altercation with Bogue, Mrs. Bement attended church services faithfully. She may even have been pleased with the Session's condemnation of slavery. Even after the confrontation in the vestibule, she directed her anger at Mr. Bogue, not at the church, by attending services when Mr. Gray officiated and absenting herself when Horace Bogue was present. We do not know the content of the notices that Mrs. Bement sought to have Bogue read, but we can guess that they were announcements of upcoming abolition meetings, and that she may have been content with a statement from the pulpit of the time and place of their occurrence.

Mrs. Bement's strategy in bearing witness to her moral convictions is most clear in her actions at communion. Along with many of her friends, she refused the communion cup because she believed it a sin to consume distilled spirits for any purpose. She had not partaken of the communion wine for nearly two years, she told Elder Forman, "believing that the fruit of the vine only was to be used as the emblem." Yet, significantly, Mrs. Bement did not protest against those who drank the wine, except with her persistent and visible refusal to accept the cup. She sought to convince her fellow communicants by example; voluntarism was clearly preferred over confrontation and coercion. That Session members were aware of Mrs. Bement's actions in dividing the Lord's Supper by partaking the bread and refusing the cup, is equally evident. Elder Forman testified that he knew the difficulty "under which Mrs. Bement laboured" and had advised her not to "wound her conscience in what she did, but had subsequently tried to show her her duty." Such ambivalent counsel was scarcely calculated to get Mrs. Bement to change her ways. Elder Cornelius Hood, who had seen Mrs. Bement refuse the cup, did not even try to "show her her duty":

Question: "Did you ever converse with Mrs. Bement on this subject?"
Answer: "I have and the reason given by her was she has scruples of conscience and that she did not think it contained the fruit of the vine and if it was it contained alcohol or some kind of drug."
Question: "Have you yourself or do you know of any other one who has ever visited with Mrs. Bement to converse with her on this particular subject before the commencement of this prosecution?"
Answer: "I do not."

United on the evils of alcohol, the elders, the minister, and Mrs. Bement had tacitly agreed to a laissez-faire approach to the communion wine. The charge against Mrs. Bement was probably Horace Bogue's way of piling transgression upon transgression, to convince the Session of her guilt by the sheer quantity of her deviations. It is important to note that only Rhoda Bement was accused of this particular heresy, although Eleanor Lum, Delia Matthews, and Prudence Douglass admitted during the course of the trial that they too had spurned the wine. Everyone managed to hold fast to principle, while living together as Christians, without compromise *or* contentiousness.

In responding to charges of unchristian behavior, Mrs. Bement pursued a legalistic defense, ingenious, to be sure, and even defiant, but with an apparent reluctance to counterattack by condemning church practices. She insisted that it was Horace Bogue, not she, who was dividing the church: the trial, she charged, looked "more like an attempt to crush than to reclaim an erring member." By demonstrating that the altercation in the vestibule was a "private transaction," overheard by no one, in which a communicant courteously and rationally questioned her minister, Mrs. Bement hoped to place blame for the controversy upon Bogue. Instead of denouncing her accusers, she sought to escape trial through a technicality. If the dispute were "private," then the fact that no one had labored with Mrs. Bement before making formal charges rendered her innocent according to the Book of Discipline of the Presbyterian church. Miss Denison testified that she did not hear Mrs. Bement's comments to the minister, although she was closer to the pair than anyone else, but the Session discounted the claims of a relative in favor of assertions that several people heard the conversation. However it began, the Session concluded that the controversy stained the reputation of the church.

Mrs. Bement's defense, whatever its merits, was not calculated to make the trial a referendum on abolition or alcohol. Most of the testimony was designed to prove that the communion wine was (or was not) alcoholic in content, or that Abby Kelley's lecture was (or was not) a Christian discourse. Criticism of the church was muted, and often inadvertent. Several Seneca Falls abolitionists, however, advanced a different view of the trial. In a letter to Abby Kelley they admitted that most of the testimony was "on one side," but insisted that the trial was having "some influence" in their town and in nearby Waterloo. These radicals reported that:

> An immense amount of testimony was taken and the attempt to represent Miss Kelley unfavorably upon the record was an entire failure. On the contrary a large number testified as to the good character of the speaker and of her speeches. The trial was pretty well attended and some of the scenes were indescribably rich, for instance—

Miss Fanny Sackett was enquired of about the terms of a pledge said to be circulated by Miss Kelley. She would not answer particularly as to its contents. She was then asked did you sign it. No. Why not? Because I did not feel ready to come out from this church. Did the pledge require you to come out of *this* church? No, not in terms, but I considered that it required those who signed it to come out of all pro slavery churches and *I considered this a pro slavery church*. Remark by a member of the Session. *The poison has gone deeper than the surface*—by the moderator I do not like to hear abolition called poison. Mrs. Perry was enquired of whether she attended the Sunday lecture. Answer she did. Were your views upon the sinfulness of slavery changed by that lecture? Answer they were. What were your views upon the subject before you heard that lecture. I can't say I had distinct views upon the subject. *Our ministers never preached anything about it* and I hardly knew that slavery *was* sinful. This was supposed by some to be a severer rebuke than any given by Abby Kelley herself. Col. Vanalstine was asked his opinion about the character and influence of the lectures. He thought it good, it served to convince him at any rate. He went there opposed to abolition agitation but was converted. He had been learned that the bible justified slavery but Miss Kelley had disabused his mind upon the subject and he had a higher respect for the bible than before.

The radicals took further solace in Mrs. Bement's appeal of her suspension to the Presbytery. Although the Session's decision was sustained, a "good audience attended," and two members of the Presbytery voted to restore Mrs. Bement. Most important, the radicals informed Miss Kelley, "more good was probably done by the spirit *of the devil exhibited* by the clerical members of that body than they have ever done by their preaching."[31]

The Seneca Falls radicals may have convinced themselves and Abby Kelley that the trial had bared the perfidy of the church, but their reading of the evidence seems strained. Mrs. Perry, Fanny Sackett, and Thomas Van Alstyne were bit players in this drama, and their asides were neither echoed nor

[31]Ansel Bascom, Edward Lyon, Abram Failing to Abby Kelley, February 16, 1844, Abby Kelley and Stephen Foster Papers, American Antiquarian Society, Worcester, Massachusetts. The quotations are from Bascom's portion of the joint letter.

sustained, even by the key defense witnesses, Elias Denison, Eleanor Lum, Jabez and Delia Matthews. Moreover, the comments of the moderator, as quoted by the radicals, suggest that Rev. Samuel Gridley was sympathetic to abolitionism. Evidently, Gridley saw no conflict between disapproval of Mrs. Bement's activities and his antislavery sentiments. If Mrs. Bement's aim had been to goad the Session to exhibit "the spirit of the devil," she was singularly unsuccessful.

The subsequent fate of the participants in the trial reminds us that divisiveness exacted a serious cost from the church, but also suggests an ongoing concern for unity even in times of great stress. Horace Bogue survived the challenge to his authority and served the Seneca Falls Presbyterian Church as minister until 1850. The Session records do not indicate any further controversy over abolition or communion wine during his tenure. Rhoda Bement, as we have seen, lost her appeal to the Presbytery and was excommunicated by the Presbyterian church. Unlike her spiritual sister Anne Hutchinson, however, Bement did not lead a band of followers into the ultraist camp of Wesleyan Methodism. Charged with neglect of ordinances, Jeremy Bement asked for a letter of dismission, presumably to join his wife, but the Session refused, because his request contained "implied charges." In his reply Bement made no mention of slavery or communion, but made the curious argument that others had neglected ordinances more than he, and charged that Horace Bogue was a slanderer. The Session declared the charge "improper to be introduced," suspended, and then excommunicated Bement. Jabez and Delia Matthews, who also attended Kelley's lecture, neglected ordinances out of sympathy for Bement. The Session showed its willingness to compromise, dropping the charges against the couple because they had been out of town when accused of absenting themselves from church. An investigation was ordered, probably to assess the willingness of the couple to return to fellowship. In September 1845 the Matthews capitulated and acknowledged that "they had done wrong": "If they had understood their obligations to the church they never would have done what they did." The Session accepted this confession and granted the Matthews dismission to the Congregational Church of Pratts-burgh. Eleanor Lum, who had in the interim become a Millerite, neglected ordinances as she awaited the end of the world, but the Session merely admonished and "affectionately exhorted her to return to her duty." Only after she refused to receive a church committee early in 1846 was she excommunicated.[32]

The only other casualty of the Bement affair was Elder Daniel W. Forman. A prominent businessman and active abolition-ist in Seneca Falls, Forman may well have been the author of the resolution on slavery passed by the Session in October 1843. The elder was probably proud of his role in putting the church on record in condemnation of the "peculiar institution," and must have felt caught in the middle of the dispute between Bement and Bogue. Forman obviously sympathized with Be-ment, but hoped to avoid having to criticize the church or its minister, especially during the time he thought his views on slavery were beginning to have an impact on the Session. It is worth emphasizing that Forman's views on slavery were no dif-ferent from Mrs. Bement's. Yet Daniel Forman's ultraism was compatible with his effort to convert the church to abolitionism from within. Once the trial began, however, neither the Session nor Mrs. Bement would let him off the hook. When the Session refused to allow Jeremy Bement to serve as counsel for his wife, Mrs. Bement asked that Forman represent her. The em-barrassed elder started the trial, but then, citing ill health, he asked to be excused. The Session granted his request, but re-fused to accede to his desire to be excused from voting on the specifications against Mrs. Bement. Forman's loyalty to the

[32]Session Minutes, First Presbyterian Church of Seneca Falls, January 1, 1845, February, 11, 1845, February 12, 1845, January 9, 1846 (*in re* J. Bement); January 10, 1845, February 12, 1845, September 12, 1845 (*in re* the Matthews); January 10, 1845, February 12, 1845, January 9, 1846 (*in re* Lum), M and UA, CU. A year passed between the suspension and excommunication of Jeremy Bement. Did the church somehow hope that Bement would repent and return, and perhaps bring his wife with him?

church was by now also on trial. The elder ultimately adjudged Mrs. Bement guilty on all charges, except unchristian conduct in the church vestibule. His was the lone dissent, however, against the Session's punishment by suspension. We should note, in this context, that Cornelius Hood, although a prominent Seneca Falls abolitionist, voted to suspend Rhoda Bement. For Hood, even more than for Forman, abolition was not on trial and the price of schism was too great.

For some Session members Forman's actions made him "unacceptable" as elder. Although a resolution to this effect was laid on the table, Forman recognized that his influence in the church had been seriously diminished. He requested a letter from the church to enable him to withdraw to the Wesleyan Methodists "in an orderly way." The Session asked the Presbytery for advice, was told that no letters could be sent to rival denominations, permitted Forman to withdraw, and struck him from the membership list.[33]

That the church sought to avoid further disruptions became apparent in the months following the Bement trial.[34] We have already noted that the committee empowered to investigate those who had neglected ordinances refused to name names, and asked for the kindness and patience of the Session with their brethren. Another committee, asked to labor with Presbyterians who had attended Abby Kelley's lecture, returned with the recommendation that the matter be dropped. Although the committee reported that "a part of such persons have not been visited," it asserted that "with the exception of a very few,"

[33]Session Minutes, First Presbyterian Church of Seneca Falls, September 27, 1844, January 10, 1845, February 11, 1845, February 12, 1845, M and UA, CU.

[34]I have found only one Presbyterian who cited the church's stance on slavery as the reason for his neglect of ordinances. Abram Failing was accused of "covenant-breaking" on September 25, 1843. Failing explained that he had been in Texas for two years, asserted that he wished to rejoin the church but would not do so if convinced that the church was pro-slavery. The church suspended Failing but waited more than two years before excommunicating him. As with Bement and the Matthewses, the Session may have hoped that Failing could be reclaimed.

those that had been labored with "have given such satisfaction as this committee and such as this session should be satisfied with." The committee did not identify the "very few" who did not give satisfaction and the Session was only too happy to comply with the suggestion that the committee be disbanded.[35]

The Presbyterian Church of Seneca Falls had endured, not because its members, ultraist or moderate, compromised their principles, but because they weighed their differences against a broader community of interest in a town of unrepentant sinners. Its experience was no doubt repeated in countless other churches in the Burned-Over District and throughout the nation. In many instances communicants found a variety of ways, short of schism, to bear witness to their convictions, to satisfy conscience without being contentious. At times, as with Rhoda Bement, a parting of the ways occurred, but most Christians were reluctant belligerents who knew the cost of undermining the unity and strength of their church.

[35]Session Minutes, First Presbyterian Church of Seneca Falls, March 15, 1844, M and UA, CU.

Index

References to illustrations are printed in italics

Index

Index

Kelley, Abigail (*cont.*)
and American Colonization Society,
43–44
and anticlericalism, 62, 111, 119–122,
165
and Rev. Horace P. Bogue, 50, 118,
120–122, 162
and disfellowship, 160, 162
and effect of lectures in Seneca Falls, 41
elected to committee of Massachusetts
Anti-Slavery Society, 67, 70, 73
and Grimké sisters, 43–44
lectures of in Seneca Falls, 16, 41, 49–50,
96, 99, 108, 110–124, 161–162, 164
and letter from Seneca Falls
Abolitionists, 164–165
and Dr. William Swan Plumer, 121–122
and Dr. James Richards, 123
as threat to authority, 36–37, 161
and women's rights, 57
King, William, 22, 84
Knapp, Rev. Joseph, 36

Labor, first step of, 96–97, 110, 122n, 164
committee report on, 139–140
Latham, Edward S., 53, 55
Lindsley, Elbert, 83
Lindsley, Mrs. *See* Freeland, Sally
Liquor licensing, 54–56, 158–159
Lum, David B., 22, 84
Lum, Eleanor, 84, 162–163, 166–167
testimony of, 107–110, 121, 132–135
Lyons, N.Y., 20
First Presbyterian Church of, 155

Marshall, Chauncey, 24, 29
Massachusetts Abolition Society, 73
Matthews, Delia, 84, 163, 165–167
testimony of, 106–107
Matthews, Jabez, 84–85, 166–167
and communion wine, 51
participant in Kelley lecture, 113
and Presbyterian attitudes toward
women, 116–117
questioned by Presbyterian Session
regarding women's place, 58
testimony of, 116–117, 122–123
McAlister, Hugh, 22, 85, 89, 100–101, 139
McAlister, Hugh Jr., 85
confrontation between Bogue and
Bement, witness of, 93
testimony of, 124–127
Mechanic's Hall, Seneca Falls, 27
Metcalf, Jonathan, 19n, 85
testimony of, 108, 112–115, 135–136
Metcalf, Joseph, 19n
Metcalf, Willard, 19n
Methodist Church, General Conference, 47

Methodist Church, Genesee Annual
Conference of, 48
Methodist Conference of Seneca Falls. *See*
Methodist Episcopal Church of Seneca
Falls
Methodist Episcopal Church of Seneca
Falls, 27, 65, 135, 157, 160
and antislavery, 45–48, 144
and communion wine, 108
and Methodist Church Genesee Annual
Conference, 48
and opposition to General Conference of
Methodist Church, 47
and resolution opposing southern
conferences on slavery, 46–47
size of membership, 148
Miller, Josiah T., 33, 53
Millerites. *See* Baptist Church of
Seneca Falls
and church schism, 156
Milling, flour, 21–25, 74
Mills, Flavius J., 51
Miyakawa, T. Scott, 145n, 151
Moderator of Presbyterian Church, 88
Moral absolutism, *See* Abolition;
Disfellowship; Immediatism;
Teetotaling; Ultraism
Mott, Lucretia, 65
Mynderse, Wilhelmus, 22, 27

Newark, N.Y., First Baptist Church of,
152–153
New Measures. *See* Presbyterian Church in
the United States of America
New School Presbyterians. *See* Presbyterian
Church in the United States of
America
New York Evangelist, 45–46, 90
New York Observer, 45–46, 90

Offense. *See Constitution of the Presbyterian
Church in the United States of America*
Old School Presbyterians. *See* Presbyterian
Church in the United States of
America
"Old Stone Shop," 20–21, 68
Ordinances, neglect of, 97, 151–154, 161,
166–168

Paine, Thomas J., 85
testimony of, 117–118
Panic of 1837, 20, 25, 42–43
Perry, Mrs. Cornelia, 41, 85, 165
testimony of, 121
Perry, Henry, 85
Phelps, Rev. Amos, 73
Pinney, Rev. E. R., 144

174

Index

Revivalism (*cont.*)
  and reform, 39–43, 157, 159–160
  in Seneca Falls, 35–36
Richards, Dr. James, 123, 132–136
Romulus, N.Y., Presbyterian Church of, 147
Rose, N.Y., Presbyterian Church of, 157
Ruling elders of the Presbyterian Church, 88

Sabbatarianism, 44
Sackett, Fanny, 86, 165
  testimony of, 110–112, 133–134
Sackett, Gary V., 22, 26–29, 69
Sackett, William, 86
St. John, Josiah, 152
Schism in churches, 143–144, 156–157, 160–161, 168
Sears, "Elder," 156
Seneca-Cayuga Canal, 71–75. *See also* Seneca Lock Company
Seneca County Agricultural Society, 27
Seneca Falls, N.Y., 15–17, *28, 67, 69, 71–74,* 149
  and the antislavery and abolition movements, 41, 45–48, 50
  and churches. *See individual denominations*
  and Erie Canal, 30
  and immigration, 30–31, 149–150
  incorporation of, 24
  and national economy, 31
  and Panic of 1837, 20, 31–32
  and political and economic rivalries, 27–28
  population of, 24
  and railroad, 30
  and revivalism, 35–36
  and socioeconomic change, 18–32
  and temperance, 53–56
  village leaders, 19n
  and voluntarism, 21–22
  and women's rights, 57–59, 76–77, 143
Seneca Falls, Board of Trustees, 54–56, 158
Seneca Falls Women's Rights Convention (1848), 65, 143
Seneca Falls Democrat
  and attitude toward church membership, 33
  and editor, Josiah T. Miller, 33
  quoted on Abby Kelley lecture, 50
  quoted on speculation and depression, 25–26
  and temperance rally, 53
Seneca Falls Temperance Society, 54
Seneca Farmer and Seneca Falls Advertiser, 24–25
Seneca Lock Company, 23
Session of the Presbyterian Church of

Seneca Falls, 87–88, 150, 166–167
  examination of witnesses, 102–137
Seward, William, 27
Sickels, William, 150
Silkerson, E., and wife, 154
Sons of Temperance, 51
Squires, Betsy, 86, 126–127
Squires, James, 86, 126–127
Squires, Mrs. Mark (Mary?), 86, 126–127
Squires, Nicholas, 86
Stanton, Elizabeth Cady, 65
Stevens, Luther F., 27
Sunderland, Rev. LeRoy, 47–48
Synod of the Free Presbyterian Churches in Ohio. *See* Presbyterian Church in the United States of America

Teetotalism, 52–53
Temperance, 18, 22. 36
  and Amelia Bloomer, 76
  and attitudes toward liquor, 55–56
  and Rhoda Bement, 39–40, 53, 55, 162–163
  and churches, 50–51, 159
  and coercive laws, 55–56, 158, 159n
  and crime and poverty, 51–52, 54–55
  divisiveness of, 40–41, 44, 53, 55, 56, 157–159
  and laity, 51
  and revivalism, 51
  and slavery, 51–52
  and temperance organization, 51–53, 86
  and temperance pledges in Seneca Falls, 54, 158
  testimony about, 102–108, 111, 119, 123–124, 137–138
  as unfair burden on community, 54–56
  and women's rights, 51–52, 76–77
  See also "Entire abstinence," Teetotalism
Thomas, John L., 157
Tillman, Andrew, 26
Timmerman, John, 53–54, 86
  and communion wine, 103–105
  and legal restrictions on retail liquor sales, 55
Transiency, 29–31, 149–150
Trial of Rhoda Bement. *See* Bement, Rhoda
  a note on the text, 87–88
Trinity Episcopal Church of Seneca Falls, 27, 118, 149
Trumansburg, N.Y., First Baptist Church of, 157

Ultraism, 41–43, 144–148, 157–158, 160–161, 166–167, 169
Universalism, 37

*Revivalism, Social Conscience, and Community
in the Burned-Over District*

Designed by Richard E. Rosenbaum.
Composed by Eastern Graphics
in 10 point Linotron 202 Baskerville, 3 points leaded,
with display lines in Baskerville.
Printed offset by Thomson/Shore, Inc. on
Warren's Number 66 Antique Offset, 50 pound basis.
Bound by John H. Dekker & Sons, Inc.

Library of Congress Cataloging in Publication Data

Main entry under title:

Revivalism, social conscience, and community in the Burned-over District.

Includes bibliographical references and index.
Contents: For the salvation of the world!: revivalism and reform in Seneca
Falls, New York / Jan M. Saltzgaber—The trial of Rhoda Bement: transcript
from the Session of the First Presbyterian Church of Seneca Falls—Varieties of
religious activity: conflict and community in the churches of the Burned-over
District / Glenn C. Altschuler.
    1. Seneca Falls (N.Y.)—Church history—Addresses, essays, lectures. 2. Re-
vivals—New York (State)—Seneca Falls—History—19th century—Addresses,
essays, lectures. 3. Seneca Falls (N.Y.)—Social conditions—Addresses, essays,
lectures. 4. New York (State)—Church history—Addresses, essays, lectures. 5.
Bement, Rhoda. I. Bement, Rhoda. II. Altschuler, Glenn C. III. Saltzgaber,
Jan M. IV. First Presbyterian Church of Seneca Falls, New York. Session.
BR560.S46R48   1983   277.47'69081   82–14296
ISBN 0–8014–1541–1 (cloth)
ISBN 0–8014–9246–7 (pbk.)